MW01381698

The Outset of Dissension in Islam

(*Islām Meiṅ Ikhtilāfāt Kā Āghāz*)

By

Ḥaḍrat Mirza Bashir-ud-Din Mahmud Ahmad

Khalīfatul-Masīḥ II, may Allah be pleased with him

ISLAM INTERNATIONAL PUBLICATIONS LTD.

The Outset of Dissension in Islam

An English rendering of *Islām Meiṅ Ikhtilāfāt Kā Āghāz,*
an urdu lecture delivered by Mirza Bashir-ud-Din Mahmud Ahmad,
Khalīfatul-Masīḥ II, may Allah be pleased with him,
The Promised Reformer and Promised Son

Translated from Urdu into English by: Atta-ur-Raḥman Khalid
Revised by: Ayyaz Mahmood Khan

First English translation published in UK: 2013

Published by
Islam International Publications Ltd.
Islamabad, Sheephatch Lane
Tilford, Surrey GU10 2AQ, UK

Printed in UK at
Raqeem Press, Tilford, UK

For further information please
or visit www.alislam.org.

ISBN: 978-1-84880-092-2

CONTENTS

About the Author vii
Foreword..ix
Necessity of Being Familiar with Islamic History 1
Importance of the Subject.. 2
Magnificent Past of Islam 3
First Devotees of Islam: Ḥaḍrat 'Uthmān[ra] & Ḥaḍrat 'Alī[ra] 4
False Narrations of Non-Muslim Historians.. 5
Companions Were Not the Real Cause of the Disorders in Islam 6
Why Dissension Emerged in the Era of the Third *Khalīfah?*...................... 8
An Introduction to Ḥaḍrat 'Uthmān[ra] 8
Status of Ḥaḍrat 'Uthmān[ra] in the Eyes of the Holy Prophet[sa] 10
What Gave Rise to the Conflict?... 11
Four Reasons for Conflict 12
The Islamic Khilāfat was a Religious Administration 14
Thinking Ill of the Companions is Without Reason................................... 16
Why Did Conflict Arise in the Era of Ḥaḍrat 'Uthmān[ra]?.......................... 22
Appointment of Abū Mūsā Al-Ash'arī[ra] as the Governor of Kufah.......... 72
Conspiracies of the Rebels Exposed.. 72
Obedience to the Ruler of the Time is Necessary...................................... 75
Another Conspiracy of the Mischief-Makers... 76
The Conspiracy Exposed 78
Ḥaḍrat 'Uthmān[ra] Summons the Mischief-Makers.................................... 78
Ḥaḍrat 'Uthmān[ra] Clears Himself of All Charges...................................... 79
Ḥaḍrat 'Uthmān[ra] Shows Mercy Towards the Mischief-Makers............... 81

Another Grave Conspiracy by the Mischief-Makers.....83
Arrival of the Mischief-Makers in Madinah.....86
The Rebels of Egypt Approach Ḥaḍrat 'Alīra.....88
The Rebels of Kufah Approach Ḥaḍrat Zubairra.....89
The Rebels of Basrah Approach Ḥaḍrat Ṭalḥahra.....89
Appointment of Muḥammad bin Abī Bakr as the Governor of Egypt....90
Reality Behind Conflicting Narrations.....90
A Golden Principle for the Verification of History.....91
Exoneration of Ḥaḍrat 'Uthmānra & the Other Companions.....92
The Rebels Enter Madinah Again.....92
The People of Madinah Advise the Rebels.....94
The Rebels Take Control of Madinah.....94
The Most Prominent Companions Ask the Rebels the Reason for their Return.....95
Ḥaḍrat 'Uthmānra Clears Himself of the Allegations Levelled by the Rebels.....96
Reality Behind the Rebel Scheme.....98
Seven Arguments in Support of the 'Letter Conspiracy'.....99
Cruelties of the Rebels upon the People of Madinah.....107
Ḥaḍrat 'Uthmānra Admonishes the Rebels.....108
The Rebels Break the Staff of the Holy Prophetsa.....109
The Rebels Pelt Stones at *Masjid-e-Nabawī* and Injure Ḥaḍrat 'Uthmānra.....110
Willingness of the Companions to Fight the Rebels.....111
Three Major Supporters of the Rebels in Madinah.....113
Ḥaḍrat 'Uthmānra is Asked to Step Down from Khilāfat.....114
The House of Ḥaḍrat 'Uthmānra Besieged.....116
Ḥaḍrat 'Alira Admonishes the Besiegers.....117
Treatment of the Rebels Towards Ḥaḍrat Ummi Ḥabībahra.....118
An Example of the Religious Indignation of Ḥaḍrat Ummi Ḥabībahra 119
Ḥaḍrat 'Ā'ishahra Prepares for Hajj.....120
Ḥaḍrat 'Uthmānra Sends a Circular to the Provincial Governors.....121
A Letter to the Pilgrims from Ḥaḍrat 'Uthmānra.....122
The Rebels Pelt Stones at the House of Ḥaḍrat 'Uthmānra.....125
Worthy Efforts of the Companions in Suppressing the Disorder.....127

The Rebels Attack the House of Ḥaḍrat 'Uthmān[ra] 130
Ḥaḍrat 'Uthmān[ra] Orders the Companions 131
Anxiety of the Rebels upon the Return of the Pilgrims 133
The Companions Fight the Rebels 135
'Abdullāh[ra] bin Salām Admonishes the Rebels 139
The Rebels Assassinate Hadrat 'Uthman[ra] 140
Events Leading up to the Martyrdom of Ḥaḍrat 'Uthmān[ra] 141
The Rebels Loot *Baitul-Māl* 144
Outrage of the Companions at the Martyrdom of Ḥaḍrat 'Uthmān[ra]. 145
Summary & Outcome of the Events Described 148

An Important Note 151
Glossary 155
Index 161

Ḥaḍrat Mirza Bashir-ud-Din Mahmud Ahmad
Khalīfatul-Masīḥ II *(may Allah be pleased with him)*

ABOUT THE AUTHOR

The Promised Son[ra] of the Promised Messiah and Mahdi[as]; the manifest Sign of Allah, the Almighty; the Word of God whose advent was prophesied by the Holy Prophet Muḥammad[sa] and the Promised Messiah[as] as well as the past Prophets; a Star in the spiritual firmament for the like of which the world has to wait for hundreds of years to appear; the man of God, crowned with a spiritual hallo from which radiated such scintillating rays of light as would instil spiritual life into his followers and captivate and enthral those who were not fortunate to follow him; an orator of such phenomenal quality that his speeches would make his audience stay put for hours on end, come rain or shine, deep into the late hours of the evenings while words flowed from his tongue like honey dripping into their ears to reach the depths of their soul to fill them with knowledge and invigorate their faith; the ocean of Divine and secular knowledge; the Voice Articulate of the age; without doubt the greatest genius of the 20th century; a man of phenomenal intelligence and memory; an epitome of the qualities of leadership; the one whose versatility cannot be comprehended—Ḥaḍrat Mirza Bashir-ud-Din Mahmud Ahmad[ra] (1889-1965), Muṣliḥ-e-Ma'ūd (the

Promised Reformer) was the eldest son and the second *Khalīfah* (successor) of the Promised Messiah[as]. He took charge of the Ahmadiyya Jamā'at at the young age of 24 when the Jama'at was still in its infancy and nourished it to its maturity for more than 50 years with his spiritual guidance, prayers, tears, toil and blood. Not only did he fortify the foundations of the Community laid down by the Promised Messiah[as], but expanded the structure of the Jamā'at by initiating various schemes, organizations, and programs taking his inspiration from the Promised Messiah[as] and under the Divine guidance. His foremost concern, to which he devoted all his life, was to accomplish the mission of the Promised Messiah[as]—the daunting task of spreading the message of true Islam in its pristine purity to the ends of the world. To achieve this, he initiated *Taḥrīk-e-Jadīd* through which spread, and continues to spread, missionary work all over the globe. His acute intelligence, keen intellect, deep and extensive scholarship and above all his God-given knowledge enabled him to produce a vast corpus of writings, speeches etc. His oeuvre is so vast that it will take many years to see the light of publication.When the Promised Messiah[as] fervently prayed to God to grant him a Sign in support of Islam, Allah gave him the good tidings about this son of his and said:

> "...He will be extremely intelligent ... and will be filled with secular and spiritual knowledge ... Son, delight of the heart, high ranking, noble; a manifestation of the First and the Last, of the True and the High; as if Allah has descended from heaven. Behold a light cometh. We shall pour our spirit into him..." [Revelation of 20th February 1886]"

FOREWORD

We are pleased to publish the English translation of a lecture delivered in urdu by Ḥaḍrat Mirza Bashir-ud-Din Mahmud Ahmad[ra], second Successor of the Promised Messiah[as], entitled, *Islām Mein Ikhtilāfāt Kā Āghāz* [The Outset of Dissension in Islam]. The lecture was delivered at the Islamiyyah College Lahore, on 26 February 1919. The primary purpose of this lecture was to provide a correct and accurate historical account of the conflicts which arose most prominently during the *khilāfat* of Ḥaḍrat 'Uthmān[ra].

The lecture is an academic masterpiece of scholarship and explains the events of the era of the third *khilāfat* in a manner that no other historian has been able to match, be it Muslim or non-Muslim.

It is an extremely significant lecture because it deals with a very important era in the history of Islam. Furthermore, the narrations, which detail the actual historical account of that era are hidden from the eyes of most people. Some historians have claimed that these conflicts arose due to the incapability of Ḥaḍrat 'Uthmān[ra], while others assert that this was the doing of various companions of the Holy Prophet[sa], due to their greed for power and political control. The lecture, however, refutes both of these two notions with ample proof and categorically establishes that conflicts arose due to the conspiracies of the enemies of Islam.

In this lecture Ḥaḍrat Mirza Bashir-ud-Din Mahmud Ahmad[ra] has shed light on the life of Ḥaḍrat 'Uthmān[ra], his piety and righteousness, and his status in the eyes of the Holy Prophet[sa]. Moreover, he has expounded upon the virtues of the companions of the Holy Prophet[sa] and has explained how these conflicts actually arose and the causes behind them. Furthermore, contrary to the belief of some historians, he has also explained that the companions of the Holy Prophet[sa] did not dislike the leadership of Ḥaḍrat 'Uthmān[ra], rather, they all loved him dearly and demonstrated an unparalleled degree of loyalty until his last breath.

Please note that, in this translation, words given in parenthesis ( ) are the words of Ḥaḍrat Khalīfatul-Masīḥ II[ra]. If any explanatory words or phrases are added by the translator for the purpose of clarification, they are put in square brackets [ ]. When this lecture was revised by Ḥaḍrat Khalīfatul-Masīḥ II[ra] for print, he added certain footnotes throughout the text of the lecture as explanatory notes, and these have been included as endnotes in the original Urdu text, in *Anwārul-'Ulūm*, volume 4, published by the Faḍl-e-'Umar Foundation. We have included all of these endnotes as footnotes throughout the English text. All additional footnotes, which have been added by the publishers are marked [Publishers]. All references, unless otherwise specified, are from the Holy Quran. Biblical references are from the King James version.

It was imperitive that an English translation of this lecture be rendered for both Muslims and non-Muslims alike, because it deals with a significant and tragic era in the history of Islam. Furthermore, since such obscurity and ambuiguity surrounds the events of that era, it was necessary that the true events be brought to light. Ḥaḍrat Khalīfatul-Masīḥ II[ra] has explained these events in a beautiful, eloquent and simple manner. It is also worthy of note that when this lecture was delivered, the attendees were college students; therefore, Ḥaḍrat Khalīfatul-Masīḥ II[ra] has taken great care to explain these events in the form of a simple and interesting narrative.

The English translation of this lecture was first rendered by Atta-ur-Rahman Khalid and was then revised and prepared for print by Ayyaz Mahmood Khan. We are also indebted to the Research Cell, Rabwah, who checked and verified the various references provided in the text. May Allah reward them all abundantly for their efforts. *Āmīn!*

Munir-ud-Din Shams
Additional Wakīlut-Taṣnīf
London, United Kingdom
July 2013

بِسْمِ اللّٰهِ الرَّحْمٰنِ الرَّحِيْمِ ۔ [1]

نَحْمَدُهٗ وَنُصَلِّيْ عَلٰى رَسُوْلِهِ الْكَرِيْمِ ۔ [2]

A lecture delivered by
Ḥaḍrat Mirza Bashir-ud-Din Mahmud Ahmad,
Khalīfatul-Masīḥ II[ra]*, Head of the Worldwide Ahmadiyya Muslim Jamā'at (1914-1965), delivered on 26th February 1919 in a gathering at the 'Martin Historical Society, Islamiyyah College, Lahore', Pakistan*

NECESSITY OF BEING FAMILIAR WITH ISLAMIC HISTORY

A short while ago I received the news, with great pleasure, that a society has been established in the Lahore Islamiyyah College in which those who are acquainted with historical facts will present their research. I was overjoyed by this, as familiarization with history acts as a great stimulant in the progress of nations. A nation that is unacquainted with its historical accounts can never advance towards progress. Knowledge of the circumstances of one's forefathers guides a person to many higher objectives. Thus, when I came to know of the establishment of this society, I was pleased by the thought that lectures on Islamic history would be delivered alongside other lectures on various historical topics. These lectures would

1. In the name of Allah, the Gracious, the Merciful [Publishers]
2. We praise Allah and invoke blessings upon his Noble Messenger [Publishers]

enable college students to understand the kinds of challenging tasks their forefathers were confronted with and the exceptional ability and perseverance with which they carried them out. They will come to know of the ancestors they have descended from and the obligations that fall upon them in their capacity as their children and representatives. They will aspire to be like their forefathers upon witnessing their magnificent deeds and their lofty splendour. Truly, I am overjoyed by the establishment of this society. Now that I have been asked to deliver a lecture on this forum regarding an aspect of Islamic history, I most delightedly postponed my departure and accepted to present my research before you on this occasion, with respect to certain subjects of historical importance.

IMPORTANCE OF THE SUBJECT

I was asked to speak on a few historical issues concerning Islam. Undoubtedly, the most significant era in Islamic history is that in which the Holy Prophet[sa], under the command of God the Exalted, presented the religion of Islam to the world. He imprinted its reflection upon the hearts of hundreds of thousands of men through twenty three years of arduous labour, and created a community of thousands of men whose thoughts, speech and actions became [an embodiment of] Islam itself. However, the foundation for dissension in Islam was laid fifteen years after the demise of the Holy Prophet[sa]. After this time, the cracks of schism between the Muslims continued to widen. The history of this very era is concealed in heavy veils of darkness. According to the opponents of Islam this is a hideous blemish upon Islam and even to its friends, serves as a perplexing question. Only a few have sought to cross the swamp of the history of that era safe and sound, and who were able to succeed in their objective. It is for this reason that I have decided to speak to you on this very topic.

MAGNIFICENT PAST OF ISLAM

As you may be aware, the task which has been assigned to me by God the Exalted (i.e., to train the Ahmadiyya Community, manage its needs and plan for its progress), in its nature, encompasses many aspects. Hence, for the purpose of its administration, it is absolutely imperative for me to possess knowledge of the historical subjects which specifically relate to the era of *Khilāfat*. For this reason, despite having little time to spare, I am compelled to keep the history of that era under study. Although our primary task is to investigate and deeply contemplate upon religion, but along with this study, by the grace of God, such hidden aspects of the history of early Islam have been disclosed to me which most people of the current age are unaware of. Due to this unfamiliarity, some Muslims are even becoming averse to their own religion. They see their past as being so dreadful that in its presence, they cannot hope for a glorious future. However, their despair is ill-founded and such views are false, and are merely due a lack of knowledge in true Islamic history. For Islam's past is so magnificent and spotless and all those trained in the company of the Holy Prophet[sa] were people of such high moral excellence that their likes cannot be found in any nation of the world, even if such people had lived in the company of a prophet. It is only those who enjoyed the company of the Holy Prophet[sa] about whom it can be said that by following the footsteps of their teacher and master, they developed such spirituality, that despite susceptible to the dangerous maze of politics they did not let virtue and honesty slip their hands. Even under the burden of [holding positions] in sovereignty, their backs remained as firm as they were at the time when they once required the basic means of sustenance and their floor was the bare earth of *Masjid-e-Nabawī*;[3] their own hands served as pillows, their occupation was listening to the blessed words of the Holy Prophet[sa] and their leisure was the worship of the One God.

FIRST DEVOTEES OF ISLAM: ḤAḌRAT 'UTHMĀN[RA] & ḤAḌRAT 'ALĪ[RA]

You have probably gathered that on this occasion, I intend to speak about the *Khilāfat* of Ḥaḍrat 'Uthmān[ra] and Ḥaḍrat 'Alī[ra]. Both of these noble men are among the first devotees of Islam. Their companions are also from among the best fruits of Islam. For a charge to be levelled against their honesty and virtue is, in reality, a disgrace upon Islam. Any Muslim who sincerely ponders over this fact will definitely reach the conclusion that in actuality, these people are above and beyond all kinds of partiality. This statement is not without foundation; rather, the pages of history are a testimony to this very fact for anyone who examines them with open eyes.

3. The Prophet's Mosque [Publishers]

FALSE NARRATIONS OF NON-MUSLIM HISTORIANS

As far as my research is concerned, whatever is alleged against these noble men and their friends is the work of the opponents of Islam. After the era of the companions, various so called Muslims, driven by their egos, have levelled allegations upon either one or the other, from among these noble men. However, despite this the truth has always prevailed and has never remained veiled in secrecy. Of course, in this era when Muslims became unfamiliar with their own history and religion, the opponents of Islam either singled out narrations of the enemies of Islam from the history of Islam, or derived false conclusions from true events, and crafted such works of history that would bring blame upon the companions and through them, upon Islam. At this time, since these non-Muslim historians are becoming the eyes through which Muslims behold everything, for this reason, Muslims have accepted everything they assert. Fearing the 'higher criticism' of Europe, even those who have had the opportunity to study original Arabic works of history for themselves, have considered the false and fabricated narrations upon which European writers base their research as being authentic and superior, and declared other narrations as being inaccurate. In this manner, the current age has become almost devoid of such people who have endeavoured to analyse events in their original form.

COMPANIONS WERE NOT THE REAL CAUSE OF THE DISORDERS IN ISLAM

Remember well that the notion of certain eminent companions being responsible for the disorders in Islam is absolutely false. After a collective study of the accounts of these people it cannot even be imagined that they attempted to destroy and ruin Islam for their personal interests or benefit. Those who have embarked to find causes for the emergence of dissension and discord in Islam within the community of the companions have faltered gravely. The causes of disorder arose from other quarters and the only hope for reaching an accurate conclusion is if they are investigated in these quarters. If the false narrations, which have been spread in relation to that era, are accepted as being true, not a single Companion[ra] can be absolved from having taken part in this disorder and not a single one appears to have stood firmly upon virtue and honesty. This is such an attack upon the truth of Islam, that both foundation and basis are uprooted. Ḥaḍrat Masīḥ[as] [the Messiah] states that a tree is recognised by its fruit[4] and due to these narrations, the fruits of the tree of Islam prove to be so bitter that no one would even be prepared to take them for free, let alone at an expense. However, would anyone who has studied the spiritual power of the Holy Prophet[sa] to even the slightest degree, be ready to accept such a notion? Of course not! It is far from reason to presume that such people who lived in the company of the Holy Prophet[sa]; were his eminent and devoted Companions; were very near relatives of the Holy Prophet[sa] and all of the

4. Luke (6:43-44) [Publishers]

other Companions without exception, deviated to such an extent in merely a few years that all of them fell into conflict due to personal interests, not due to religious reasons, and this misfortune shook the very core of Islam. It is unfortunate that although Muslims do not explicitly state that the companions created disorder in order to destroy and ruin Islam, but they have accepted the narrations of such people as being true, who had not fully accepted Islam and had only made a verbal declaration of faith. Then, they have relied on the research of bitter enemies of Islam who were in pursuit of its destruction. Ultimately, therefore, such people concede that the community of the companions was, God forbid, completely devoid of virtue and honesty.[5]

In my exposition, I shall bear in mind not to mention dates so that it is not difficult to understand and the subject does not become confusing. The real objective of this lecture is to familiarise college students with certain events of early Islam. For this reason, I shall also abstain from quoting Arabic quotations insofar as possible and shall describe events in the form of a narrative.

5. Whilst reviewing this article a second time for publication, I have given various references of historical importance as footnotes and in order to make the book less burdensome for those who study it, I have sufficed with the use of references from *Tārīkhuṭ-Ṭabarī* only, with a few exceptions.

WHY DISSENSION EMERGED IN THE ERA OF THE THIRD KHALĪFAH?

All educated Muslims are probably aware that signs of dissension amongst the Muslims began to prominently emerge in the era of the third *Khalīfah*. Prior to him, in the era of Ḥaḍrat Abū Bakr[ra] and Ḥaḍrat 'Umar[ra], discord never took on a serious nature. The Muslims were so united that both friend and foe believed that it was impossible to divide them. It is for this reason that people generally attribute the discord under discussion to the weakness of the third *Khalīfah*. However, as I shall explain ahead, this is not the case.

AN INTRODUCTION TO ḤAḌRAT 'UTHMĀN[RA]

After Ḥaḍrat 'Umar[ra], the gaze of all the companions fell upon Ḥaḍrat 'Uthmān[ra] for the office of *Khilāfat* and thus, he was appointed for this task through the consultation of the eminent companions. He was the son-in-law of the Holy Prophet[sa] and two daughters of the Holy Prophet[sa] were wedded to him one after another. When the second daughter of the Holy Prophet[sa] passed away, the Holy Prophet[sa] said, *"If I had another daughter I would marry her to Ḥaḍrat 'Uthmān[ra] as well."*[6] This shows that he held a special rank of honour in the sight of the Holy Prophet[sa]. He held a very unique position in the sight of the people of Makkah and was a wealthy man according to the circumstances of Arabia at the time. After Ḥaḍrat Abū Bakr[ra] accepted Islam, one of the people to whom he particularly chose

6. Usdul-Ghābah Fī Ma'rifatiṣ-Ṣaḥābah, vol. 3, p. 481, 'Uthmānubnu 'Affāna, Dārul-Fikr, Beirut, Lebanon [Publishers]

to preach the message of Islam was Ḥaḍrat 'Uthmān[ra]. The view of Ḥaḍrat Abū Bakr[ra] with respect to Ḥaḍrat 'Uthmān[ra] did not prove false and only after a few days of preaching, he accepted Islam. In this manner, he joined the *as-sābiqūnal-awwalūn*[7] or that pioneer group of Islam which the Holy Quran has praised in admirable words. The degree of honour and respect that he possessed in Arabia can be understood from the incident that when the Holy Prophet[sa] journeyed to Makkah on the basis of a vision, and the Makkans, blinded by their malice and enmity, refused to grant him permission to perform the *'umrah*,[8] the Holy Prophet[sa] proposed that an esteemed person should be sent to the Makkans to negotiate the matter. When Ḥaḍrat 'Umar[ra] was selected for this, he replied,

> *"O Messenger of Allah, I am prepared to go, but if there is anyone in Makkah who can negotiate with the Makkans then it is Ḥaḍrat 'Uthmān[ra] because he holds special regard in their eyes. Hence, if someone else were to go, there cannot be as much hope for success in him as opposed to if Ḥaḍrat 'Uthmān[ra] went."*

The Holy Prophet[sa] also considered this view as being correct and consequently sent Ḥaḍrat 'Uthmān[ra] for the task. It can be understood from this incident that Ḥaḍrat 'Uthmān[ra] was looked upon with special honour even by the disbelievers.

---

7. The foremost among the believers. [Publishers]
8. A lesser pilgrimage to the Holy Ka'bah, in which some of the rites of hajj are left out.

STATUS OF ḤAḌRAT 'UTHMĀN[RA] IN THE EYES OF THE HOLY PROPHET[SA]

The Holy Prophet[sa] held a great deal of respect for Ḥaḍrat 'Uthmān[ra]. On one occasion, the Holy Prophet[sa] was lying down when Ḥaḍrat Abū Bakr[ra] arrived, but the Holy Prophet[sa] remained lying. After some time, Ḥaḍrat 'Umar[ra] arrived, but again, he remained lying. When Ḥaḍrat 'Uthmān[ra] arrived, he instantly adjusted his clothes and said, *"There is a great deal of modesty in the disposition of Ḥaḍrat 'Uthmān[ra], and it is in consideration of his feelings that I have done this."*[9] He was one of those rare men who had never consumed alcohol and had never approached adultery even prior to accepting Islam. In the country of Arabia, where drinking alcohol was thought to be a source of pride and adultery a daily indulgence, these were qualities which could not be found in more than a handful of people before Islam. Therefore, Ḥaḍrat 'Uthmān[ra] was no ordinary man. He possessed very high moral qualities. With respect to worldly rank he was exceptional. He was the foremost in Islam. The Holy Prophet[sa] was very pleased with him. Ḥaḍrat 'Umar[ra] has declared him as being among the six men who, up to the demise of the Holy Prophet[sa], held his utmost pleasure. Furthermore, he was from among the *'asharah mubashsharah,*[10]

9. Ṣaḥīḥ Muslim, Kitābu Faḍā'iliṣ-Ṣaḥābah, Bābu Min Faḍā'ili 'Uthmānibni 'Affāna, Ḥadīth No. 6210

10. In actuality, *'asharah mubashsharah* has become a renowned term, otherwise, there were many more companions about whom the Holy Prophet[sa] had prophesied that they would enter paradise. The term *'asharah mubashsharah* refers to those ten *muhājirin*, who were a part of the *majlis-e-shūrā* [consultative body] of the Holy Prophet[sa] and who he especially trusted.

meaning he was one of those ten men about whom the Holy Prophet[sa] had given the glad tiding that they would enter paradise.[11]

For about six years after he took up the office of *Khilāfat,* no disorder of any kind arose. In fact, people were generally very pleased with him. After this, conflict suddenly arose which steadily grew so large that it could not be stopped by the efforts of any individual. Ultimately, this proved to be extremely injurious for Islam. Thirteen hundred years have passed, but its effects upon the Muslim ummah have not died away to this day.

WHAT GAVE RISE TO THE CONFLICT?

Now the question is how did this conflict come about? Some have alleged the cause to be Ḥaḍrat 'Uthmān[ra] while others, Ḥaḍrat 'Alī[ra]. Some say that Ḥaḍrat 'Uthmān[ra] introduced certain innovations in the faith, which caused an uproar among the Muslims. Others assert that Ḥaḍrat 'Alī[ra] secretly conspired to acquire *Khilāfat* and had Ḥaḍrat 'Uthmān[ra] killed by creating hostility against him so that he could become the *Khalīfah* himself. However, both of these notions are false; neither did Ḥaḍrat 'Uthmān[ra] introduce innovations in the faith, nor did Ḥaḍrat 'Alī[ra] have him killed or took part in a conspiracy to murder him in order to become the *Khalīfah* himself. In fact, there were other causes for this revolt. Ḥaḍrat 'Uthmān[ra] and Ḥaḍrat 'Alī[ra] are completely free from the blemish of such allegations. Both were very holy men. Ḥaḍrat 'Uthmān[ra] was

---

11. Sunanut-Tirmidhī, Kitābul-Manāqib, Manāqibi 'Abdir-Raḥmānibni 'Aufin, Ḥadīth No. 3747

the person about whom the Holy Prophet[sa] had said, that he had served Islam to such a great extent that now he could do whatsoever he wished, God would not question him.[12] This did not imply that he would not be held accountable even if he renounced Islam. In fact, it inferred that he had acquired so many qualities and had progressed so much in virtue that it was no longer possible for any of his actions to be in violation of the commandments of Allah the Exalted. As such, Ḥaḍrat 'Uthmān[ra] was not a man who would issue an order in violation to the shariah, nor was Ḥaḍrat 'Alī[ra] a man who would secretly conspire to assume *Khilāfat*. As far as I have contemplated and studied there are four reasons for this horrific uprising.

FOUR REASONS FOR CONFLICT

Firstly: the nature of men is generally inclined towards the acquisition of wealth and stature with the exception of those whose hearts God the Exalted has particularly cleansed. Certain people who were not complete in their faith became envious upon witnessing the honour, status, success and authority of the companions. As has been a practice since time immemorial, they began to desire that these companions resign from all their responsibilities of government and hand over positions to them so that others are given the opportunity to exhibit their skill as well. They also disliked that the companions not only held State authority but also received a special share of the riches. Hence, these people continued to burn inside with jealousy. They

12. Sunanut-Tirmidhī, Kitābul-Manāqib, Manāqibi 'Uthmānibni 'Affāna, Chapter No. 61, Ḥadīth No. 3700

awaited a revolution by which the government would crumble and fall into their hands, so that they could also demonstrate their talent and skill and gain worldly wealth and stature. In worldly States such ideas may be forgiven to some extent and can even be considered rational at times. This is because firstly, the foundation of worldly States is purely based upon apparent means; and a significant cause in the progress of apparent means is the introduction of new ideas and spirit into the governmental framework as well. This is only possible if old workers vacate their posts freely, leaving space for others.

Secondly: Since a worldly State receives authority in representation of the public it is compelled to respect the public opinion. It is also essential for those voicing the public view to possess substantial involvement in the organization of the works of the state. However, in a religious movement the matter is quite the opposite, where the overriding principle of all principles is to abide by a set law. Furthermore, the interference of one's personal ideas is strictly prohibited, except with relation to such derivative institutes of the law where the shariah has remained silent. Secondly, religious movements are afforded authority from God the Exalted, and it is the duty of people who control the reins of administration to prevent people from moving out of line in religious matters. Instead of voicing the opinions of people, it is incumbent upon them to shape the views of people into the mould that has been designed by God the Exalted according to the needs of that time.

THE ISLAMIC KHILĀFAT WAS A RELIGIOUS ADMINISTRATION

Therefore, due to not understanding the reality of Islam, such objections would arise in the hearts of those people. They failed to understand that the Islamic *Khilāfat* was no worldly government, nor were the companions ordinary chiefs of State. On the contrary, the Islamic *Khilāfat* was a religious administration which was established in accordance with the special injunctions of the Holy Quran contained in *Sūratun-Nūr*. The companions were those pillars of religion whom God the Exalted had made obligatory to follow in order to advance in spiritual ranks. The companions left their jobs and adopted every type of poverty and destitution, they placed their lives in danger; left the company and love of their close relatives and dear ones; said farewell to their homelands and sacrificed their sentiments and emotions; and adopted the company and love of the Holy Prophet[sa]. Some of them had learnt Islam lesson by lesson, spending approximately a quarter of a century as students of the Holy Prophet[sa]. Moreover, they strengthened the practical aspect of Islam by acting upon it. They understood the meaning of Islam, its purpose, its reality and how one should act upon its teachings. Additionally, they understood the benefits that could be attained by acting upon it. Hence, they were not kings and members of a worldly government; rather, they were teachers of the very last religion and law of the Seal of Prophets[sa]. It was made incumbent upon them to represent Islam through their actions, speech, and conduct, and to imprint its teaching upon the hearts of people and to make them practicing followers. They were not supporters of tyranny; rather, they were supporters of the lustrous law. They abhorred materialism. If it were up to them they would have abandoned the world and sat in places of seclusion, and eased their hearts with the remembrance of God. However, they were compelled by the responsibility which had been laid upon their shoulders by God and His Messenger[sa].[13] Therefore, whatever they did was not on account of their own desires; rather, it was in accordance with the command of God the Exalted and as per the guidance of His Messenger[sa]. Hence, it was a terrible mistake to be jealous and think ill of them. Now remains the objection that the companions were given special sums of wealth. This was also a form of mischief because whatever the companions received was in accordance to their rights. They did not usurp the rights of others in order to accumulate their own wealth. In fact, every single individual, even if he had become a Muslim one day before, received his right in the same way as pioneer believers. Of course, the efforts of the companions and their labour and sacrifice exceeded that of others. Moreover, their age-old services were in addition to all this. Hence, they deserved a greater right over others out of justice, not injustice. For this reason, they received greater remuneration in comparison to others. They had not fixed their own shares themselves; on the contrary, Allah and His Messenger had fixed their shares. If these people had not been

13. Later events of Islamic history evidently prove how beneficial and blessed the intervention of the companions truly was; by removing their intervention for a period in time, God the Exalted demonstrated the detrimental results of moving them aside. The manner in which Islam became the target of mockery at the hands of so-called Muslims is such that when a person reads these accounts, the heart trembles and the body shivers.

treated in a special manner, how would the prophecies contained in the Holy Quran and *aḥādīth* of the Holy Prophet[sa], regarding their success, prosperity, comfort and wealth have been fulfilled? If after the fall of Caesar's kingdom and victory over his treasury, Ḥaḍrat 'Umar[ra] had not given Caesar's bangles to Surāqah bin Mālik[ra], how then would the prophecy of the Holy Prophet[sa] be fulfilled in which he said, *"I see the bangles of Caesar in the hands of Surāqah."* I would also add, however, that whatever the companions received was not by usurping the rights of others. In fact, anyone who carried out even a small task in the government was given his right. The *Khulafā'* were very cautious in this regard. The companions were merely given their fair share, though undoubtedly, it was greater than that of others, due to their work and former services. Then a group of them also took part in the wars that arose at the time and in exchange of this service they were just as deserving of a reward, as were others. However, it should also be remembered, that history proves that the companions did not have the habit of saving this money or spending it on their own souls. They only accepted their share in order to prove the truth of the words of Allah and His Messenger. Each and every one of them was an unparalleled model of generosity and munificence; their wealth was spent solely for the welfare and guardianship of the poor.

THINKING ILL OF THE COMPANIONS IS WITHOUT REASON

Therefore, the jealousy and ill-will which had taken root in some people, with respect to the companions was without reason and cause. However, this seed had been sown irrespective of whether this was with or without reason. A segment of people who were unfamiliar with the reality of religion began to look upon them as if they were usurpers. They anxiously waited for an opportunity to push them aside so that they could assume control of the government and its wealth. The second reason for this disorder was that Islam had established such means of freedom of conscience and action, and equality between people, as were not even available to great philosophical thinkers before this. As is the rule, there are some, who innately possess an element of disease, and thus, suffer, instead of benefitting from even the best of nourishments. Similarly, instead of benefitting from this principle of freedom of conscience and action, some people suffered by it and were unable to remain within its boundaries. This disease began in the time of the Holy Prophet[sa] when a wretched so-called Muslim confronted him and uttered the words, *"O Messenger of Allah! Keep in mind the fear of Allah, for you have not acted with justice in the distribution of riches."* To this, the Holy Prophet[sa] replied:

اِنَّهٗ يَخْرُجُ مِنْ ضِئْضِئِ هٰذَا قَوْمٌ يَتْلُوْنَ كِتَابَ اللّٰهِ رَطْبًا لَا يُجَاوِزُ حَنَاجِرَهُمْ يَمْرُقُوْنَ مِنَ الدِّيْنِ كَمَا يَمْرُقُ السَّهْمُ مِنَ الرَّمِيَّةِ

"A nation will arise from this person's progeny that will recite the Quran often but it will not descend their throats. They will stray from faith just as an arrow misses its target."[14]

---

14. Ṣaḥīḥul-Bukhārī, Kitābul-Maghāzī, Bābu Ba'thi 'Aliyyibni Abī Ṭālibin Wa Khālidibnil-Walīdi Ilal Yamani Qabla Ḥajjatil-Wadā'i, Ḥadīth No. 4351

The latent fire of such thoughts flared up a second time in the era of Ḥaḍrat 'Umar[ra]. Once, a person stood up in the midst of a gathering and levelled an allegation against Ḥaḍrat 'Umar[ra], who was a selfless person and the guardian *Khalīfah* of the finances of the community of Prophet Muhammad[sa] saying, *"From where have you acquired this cloak?"*[15] Nevertheless, on both these occasions disorder did not take on a frightening shape because until then, neither was there any prepared ground for its growth and development, nor did a favourable climate exist. However, in the time of Ḥaḍrat 'Uthmān, may Allah be pleased with him, both these factors came to exist and this plant, which I shall call the 'plant of disorder,' strengthened on very firm foundations. In the time of Ḥaḍrat 'Alī[ra] it grew and developed to such extent that its branches well nigh extended to cover all the corners of the Muslim world under their shade. However, Ḥaḍrat 'Alī[ra] recognised the harms of this plant in good time and cut it to the ground with a fatal blow. Though he could not manage to completely wipe it out, but at least he was able to restrict its area of influence to a great extent.

In my opinion, the **third** cause was that although a large number of people had brought about a grand transformation in their lives due to the effect of the luminous rays of Islam, but this could in no way fulfil the shortcoming which always makes an individual require a teacher for the acquisition of religious and worldly knowledge. Even in the era of the Holy Prophet[sa], when people accepted Islam in troops, the very same danger

15. Al-Fakhrī fil-Ādābis-Sulṭāniyyati Wad-Duwalil-Islāmiyyah, By Muḥammad bin 'Alī bin Ṭabāṭabā, p. 29, Ad-Daulatul-Islāmiyyah, Dāru Ṣādir, Beirut [Publishers]

existed began to emerge. However, God had promised him that in this era of progress, those who would accept Islam would be safeguarded from evil influence. After his demise, although a violent wave of apostasy surged forth, it was instantly contained and people learnt of the reality of Islam. However, after the demise of the Holy Prophet[sa] when the conquests of Persia, Syria and Egypt took place, the spiritual victories, which Islam achieved due to its interaction with other religions, became the very cause for the disturbance of its political order. Millions of people entered Islam and upon witnessing its magnificent teaching, became so devoted to it that they became prepared to offer their lives. However, the number of new converts to Islam multiplied so rapidly that no satisfactory arrangement could be made for their education. As is the rule and from an in depth study of the human mind it can be concluded that due to their initial enthusiasm the need for their education and training was not felt. They imitated the Muslims completely and followed every instruction with pleasure. However, as this initial fervance began to subside, those who had not received the opportunity to undergo spiritual training began to feel as if adherence to Islamic injunctions was a burden. As soon as this new enthusiasm died down, their old habits began to re-emerge. Anyone can commit mistakes and man learns through experience. However, if these people had truly desired to gain something, then after having stumbled for a while they would have eventually learned. In the era of the Holy Prophet[sa] conditions were such, that once a person committed a crime and he himself confessed to his crime and did not fear being stoned, even after the Holy Prophet[sa] pointed out that when Allah the Exalted covers up a sin then why should one disgrace himself.[16] In contrast, now, if even the smallest punishment was imposed in order to maintain the boundaries of the shariah, these people disliked this. Hence, there were some people who would not refrain from violating the shariah because Islam had not penetrated their hearts. Moreover, when the shariah would be upheld, these very people would be infuriated and raise objections against the *Khalīfah* and his officials. In addition, they would harbour malice in their hearts against them and plot to uproot their administration altogether.

The **fourth** cause for conflict, in my view, was that Islam progressed at such an extraordinary pace that in the beginning, its opponents were unable to perceive this. The Makkans were still living under a false sense of pride over their might and thought that the Holy Prophet[sa] was weak, when Makkah was conquered and Islam spread throughout the Arab peninsula. The Caesar of Rome and Khosrau of Persia viewed this growing power of Islam with such contempt in the likeness of a spectator, just as a tyrant wrestler looks upon the first attempt of a child to stand up.

The Persian and Byzantine Empires were shattered into pieces with a single blow from the strike of the Prophet Muhammad[sa]. So long as the Muslims were engaged in confronting these tyrant governments, that had forced people into slavery for over hundreds, if not thousands of years, and their humble and ill-equipped army was at war with the massive

16. Ṣaḥīḥul-Bukhārī, Kitābul-Ḥudūd, Bābu Su'ālil-Imāmil-Muqirr, Ḥadīth No. 6825 [Publishers]

and well-equipped armies of their enemies, the opponents of Islam thought that the Muslim victories were temporary and soon this wave would take another turn; and this nation, rising in the likeness of a storm would soon fly away like a tornado. However, there astonishment knew no bounds when in a period of a few years the horizon was cleared and the banner of Islam began to flutter in all four corners of the world. This was such a triumph which left the enemy dumbfounded and it drowned in a sea of surprise and astonishment. In the eyes of enemy forces, the companions as well as those who gained their company began to appear as supernatural beings. The enemy lost all hope. However, when a period of time elapsed after these victories and their awe and astonishment lessened, and their fear lessened after meeting the Companions[as], the thought of opposing Islam and establishing false religions developed. As far as argumentation was concerned, they could not contest with the pure teachings of Islam. Governments had been wiped out and the one tool that was always used against the truth i.e., oppression and tyranny, had been destroyed. Now only one avenue remained, which was to do the work of an enemy in the guise of a friend, and through agreement, create divide. Hence, various evil people who were becoming blinded by the light of Islam accepted the religion outwardly, but actually sought to destroy it after apparently converting to Islam. Since the progress of Islam was associated with *Khilāfat*, in the presence of a shepherd, the wolf was unable to attack. Therefore, it was proposed that *Khilāfat* be wiped out and the thread of harmony which tied the Muslims of the entire world together be torn, so that the Muslims could be deprived of the blessings of unity. In this manner, false religions could once again find an avenue of progress by taking advantage of the absence of a leader and no danger would exist for their deceit and deception to be revealed.

In my opinion, these are the four causes which gave rise to the grand rebellion that shook the very foundation of the Muslim ummah in the era of Ḥaḍrat 'Uthmān, may Allah be pleased with him. There were times when the enemy was overjoyed by the thought that now, this magnificent fortress would crumble to the ground, along with its roofs and walls. This religion had foretold that it would achieve the following magnificent future:

هُوَ الَّذِيْٓ اَرْسَلَ رَسُوْلَهٗ بِالْهُدٰى وَدِيْنِ الْحَقِّ لِيُظْهِرَهٗ عَلَى الدِّيْنِ كُلِّهٖ

"He it is Who has sent His Messenger with [the guidance] and the Religion of truth, so that He may cause it to prevail of all other religions."[17]

The enemy believed that this religion would now be eradicated once and for all.

WHY DID CONFLICT ARISE IN THE ERA OF ḤAḌRAT 'UTHMĀN[RA]?

In light of the historical events which transpired in the last days of the *Khilāfat* of Ḥaḍrat 'Uthmān[ra], I have deduced the actual causes of this conflict and presented them before you. You shall understand for yourself as to whether they are correct or incorrect, once you become aware of the events from which I have drawn this conclusion. However, before I allude

17. As-Saff (61:10)

to these events I wish to say something with regards to the question of why unrest arose in the time of Ḥaḍrat 'Uthmān[ra]? The fact of the matter is that in the time of Ḥaḍrat 'Uthmān[ra], people entered Islam in large numbers. The vast majority of these new Muslims were unfamiliar with the Arabic language, thus, learning the Islamic faith was not as easy for them as it was for the Arabs. For centuries, due to their interaction with the Persians and Syrians, even those who knew Arabic, had remained victim to the filthy views which were a natural result of the civilisation of that era. In addition to this, due to battles with the Persians and Christians, the full strength of most companions and those who followed him, was being exhausted in warding off the onslaughts of the enemy. Two major causes for why new Muslims were unable to become as familiar with Islam as was required, were that on the one hand, Muslim attention was occupied by external enemies and, on the other hand, new Muslims were unfamiliar with the Arabic language or had been influenced by non-Arab views. In the era of Ḥaḍrat 'Umar[ra], since the Muslims were engaged in a large-scale series of wars and the danger of the enemy remained ever-present, people did not receive an opportunity to contemplate other matters. Additionally, due to being in constant battle with the enemy, naturally, religious passion would rise up again and again, and this covered up the weakness in religious knowledge which existed among the people. The same conditions were prevalent even in the early era of Ḥaḍrat 'Uthmān[ra]. On one hand, wars ensued, while earlier influences also remained in the hearts of people. When a state of peace prevailed to some extent and initial enthusiasm also subsided, it was then that this religious weakness began to show its colours. The enemies of Islam capitalised on this opportunity and mobilised in order to create mischief. Hence, this disorder was not the result of any action of Ḥaḍrat 'Uthmān[ra]. As a matter of fact, had these conditions developed in the time of any *Khalīfah*, disorder would have emerged. The only fault of Ḥaḍrat 'Uthmān[ra] was that he was elected to the office of *Khilāfat* at a time when his involvement in creating disorder was no greater than that of Ḥaḍrat Abū Bakr[ra] or Ḥaḍrat 'Umar[ra]; and who can say that this conflict was the result of a weakness on the part of these two holy men? It does not cease to amaze me as to how certain people assert that these disorders were the result of a weakness of Ḥaḍrat 'Uthmān[ra]. Ḥaḍrat 'Umar[ra], who could not have even imagined that Ḥaḍrat 'Uthmān[ra] would become *Khalīfah*, had already identified the root cause of this conflict in the era of his own *Khilāfat*. He then warned the Quraish in this regard with strong words. As such, it is written that Ḥaḍrat 'Umar[ra] would not allow the senior companions to go forth for war and if they sought his permission he would say, *"Is the jihad which you performed alongside the Holy Prophet[sa] not sufficient?"*[18] Once, when the companions finally complained, he said:

"I have grazed Islam just as a camel is grazed. First, a

---

18. Ḥaḍrat 'Umar[ra] had two reasons in view. Firstly, this meant that a community of teachers always remained in Madinah. Secondly, the companions received special shares from *baitul-māl* [national treasury] due to their being the foremost in belief and offering services in the era of the Holy Prophet[sa]. Thus, Ḥaḍrat 'Umar thought that if these people had also taken part in expeditions, they would have received even more shares and this would be difficult for others to bear.

camel is born, then it becomes a calf. Then it grows two teeth, then four teeth and then six. Then it grows canine teeth. Now, what can be expected for one whose canine teeth have grown except for weakness. Listen! Islam has now reached its perfection. The Quraish desire that they should take all the wealth for themselves, while others are deprived.[19] *Hearken! Until 'Umar bin Al-Khaṭṭāb is alive, he shall hold the Quraish by their necks so that they do not fall into the fire of disorder."*[20]

It appears from this statement of Ḥaḍrat 'Umar[ra], that even in his own era, he noticed the views billowing in the minds of people that the companions received a greater share. For this reason, except for a few companions, without whom the armies could not be managed, he would not allow the companions to go forth for jihad so that people would not be put to trial due to the Companions receiving a double share. Moreover, he felt that Islam had now reached the pinnacle of its success and after this, only the danger of its decline remained, not a hope of further progress.

After having mentioned this much, I shall now relate the sequence of events which shed light on the reality of the conflicts that arose in the time of Ḥaḍrat 'Uthmān[ra].

I have already mentioned that in the beginning of the *Khilāfat* of Ḥaḍrat 'Uthmān[ra] we see no sign of disorder for up to six years. Quite the contrary, it appears that people were

19. In other words, if the companions took a share for being pioneers and then also for now taking part in jihad, others would receive less.

20. Tārīkhuṭ-Ṭabarī, vol. 5, pp. 184-185, Dhikru Ba'di Siyari Uthmāna....., Published by Dārul-Fikr, Beirut, 2002 edition

generally pleased with him.[21] In fact, it is ascertained from history that in this era he was even dearer to the people than Ḥaḍrat 'Umar[ra]. Not only was he dear to the people, in fact, they were in awe of him. A poet of that era testifies to this fact in his poetic verses, in the following words:[22]

> *"O rebellious people! Do not loot and devour the people's wealth in the reign of 'Uthmān[ra]; for Ibni 'Affān is he whom you have experienced. In accordance with Quranic injunctions, he executes those who pillage; he has always been a guardian of the injunctions of this Holy Quran; he is the one who teaches the people to act upon these injunctions."*[23]

However, after six years, we see a campaign in the seventh year; and this was not directed against Ḥaḍrat 'Uthmān[ra]; rather, it was directed against the companions or against various governors. As such, Ṭabarī narrates that Ḥaḍrat 'Uthmān[ra] took full consideration of the rights of people. However, those people who did not enjoy the distinction of being the foremost pioneers in Islam did not receive the same level of honour as the early and pioneer Muslims did in gatherings; nor did they receive an

---

21. Tārīkhuṭ-Ṭabarī, vol. 5, pp. 101-102, Dhikru Mā Kāna Fīhā Minal-Aḥdāthil-Mashhūrah, Published by Dārul-Fikr, Beirut, 2002 edition

22. لَا تَأْكُلُوْا اَبَداً جِيْرَانَكُمْ سَرَفاً   اَهْلُ الدَّعَارَةِ فِىْ مُلْكِ ابْنِ عَفَّانَ
اِنَّ ابْنَ عَفَّانَ الَّذِىْ جَرَّبْتُمْ   فَطِمُ اللَّصُوْصِ بِحُكْمِ الْفُرْقَانِ
مَا زَالَ يَعْمَلُ بِالْكِتٰبِ مُهَيْمِنًا   فِىْ كُلِّ عُنْقٍ مِنْهُمْ وَبَنَان

23. Tārīkhuṭ-Ṭabarī, vol. 5, pp. 104-105, Dhikrus-Sababi Fī 'Azli....., Published by Dārul-Fikr, Beirut, 2002 edition

equal share in rule and wealth. Over time, some people began to criticise this superiority and deemed it to be an injustice. However, these people feared the Muslim masses and out of their fear that the people would oppose them, they would not express their views. Instead, the practice which they had employed was to secretly incite people against the companions. When they came across an uneducated Muslim or a freed Bedouin slave, they would open up their book of complaints. Consequently, either out of ignorance or due to their own desire for position, certain people would join them. Gradually, this group began to multiply and reached a large number.[24]

When disorder is about to arise, its contributing factors also begin to accumulate in an extraordinary manner. On the one hand, those of a jealous disposition were beginning to grow incensed against the companions. On the other hand, the zeal for Islam, which is usually present in the hearts of all those who convert from other religions, began to decline amongst these new Muslims, who had neither lived in the company of the Holy Prophet[sa], nor had they received an opportunity to spend a great deal of time with those who had been in his company. As a matter of fact, as soon as they accepted Islam, it was their presumption that they had learned everything. As soon as this Islamic fervour lessened, the control which Islam possessed over their hearts also began to fall weak. They, once again, began to enjoy committing the sins that they had once indulged in before they became Muslims. When they were punished for their

24. Tārīkhuṭ-Ṭabarī, vol. 5, pp. 108-110, Dhikrus-Sababi Fī 'Azli....., Published by Dārul-Fikr, Beirut, 2002 edition

crimes, instead of reforming themselves, they became bent upon the destruction of those who were administering these sentences. Ultimately, they proved to become the cause of creating a great rift in the unity enjoyed by Islam. The centre of these people was in Kufah. However, the strangest thing to note is that an incident took place in Madinah itself, which demonstrates that in that time, some people were as unfamiliar with Islam as the ignorant people of today who live in the remotest areas. Ḥimrān bin Abbān was a person who married a woman during her *'iddat.*[25] When Ḥaḍrat 'Uthmān, may Allah be pleased with him, learned of this, he was displeased at him; not only did he order a separation, but also exiled him from Madinah to Basrah.[26] This occurrence demonstrates how certain people began to perceive that the mere acceptance of Islam authorized them as being scholars of Islam. They did not feel a need for further research. Perhaps, due to an influence of various views, related to believing in unlawful things as being permissible, they deemed it a futile act to follow the shariah. This is a sole event and perhaps in Madinah, which was the centre of Islam, there was no one else who was as ignorant as he. However, in other cities, there were some who continued to advance in sins. Hence, it is ascertained from the circumstances of Kufah that a band of youths had taken root for the purpose of robbery. It is written that once they proposed robbing the house of a person named 'Alī bin

---

25. A fixed time period specified by the Islamic shariah, which must elapse before a widow or divorced lady is permitted to marry again. [Publishers]
26. Tārīkhuṭ-Ṭabarī, vol. 5, p. 139, Dhikrul-Khabari 'An Tasyīri 'Uthmāna....., Published by Dārul-Fikr, Beirut, 2002 edition

Ḥaisumān Al-Khuzā'ī. They broke into his house at night, but he learned of this and came out with a sword. However, when he saw a large party he raised a hue and cry. At this, the group said, *"Quiet! Or we shall wipe out your fear with a single blow,"* and they killed him. During this time, the neighbours had become alert; they gathered around and apprehended the robbers. A Companion named Ḥaḍrat Abū Shuraiḥ, may Allah be pleased with him, who was a neighbour of this person and had witnessed the whole incident from over the wall of his house, testified that, in fact, these people had killed 'Alī. Similarly, his son also testified. The matter was submitted to Ḥaḍrat 'Uthmān[ra] in writing and he sentenced all of them to death. Hence, Walīd bin 'Utbah, who had been appointed as the governor of Kufah by Ḥaḍrat 'Uthmān[ra] in those days, executed all these robbers in an open plain beyond the gate of the city.[27] Apparently, this seems to be an insignificant event, but if one studies the conditions of that time, this was not an minor incident. With the progress of Islam, the rate of crime died out completely. People were at such peace that they did not even fear sleeping with open doors. Ḥaḍrat 'Umar[ra] had even stopped his governors from making security posts outside their offices. Although, the intention of Ḥaḍrat 'Umar[ra] in this was to facilitate the people in submitting their complaints to governors with ease, this order could only have been carried out until an extreme level of peace prevailed. This incident was also especially worthy of note because the children of various powerful and influential people, who

27. Tārīkhuṭ-Ṭabarī, vol. 5, p. 104, Dhikrus-Sababi Fī 'Azli....., Published by Dārul-Fikr, Beirut, 2002 edition

possessed control in their respective spheres, were involved in this robbery. As such, this was not an ordinary crime; in fact, it was the foreshadowing of a great revolution. What else could this have been an indication towards other than the fact that the control of Islam upon the hearts of people who were unfamiliar with the religion of Islam was beginning to diminish? They were reverting to their old habits once again. Not only the poor, but even the rich were rising up to gain back their lost glory through murder and bloodshed. The Companion, Ḥaḍrat Abū Shuraiḥ[ra], gathered this very well; he instantly sold his wealth, etc., and leaving Kufah, returned to Madinah along with his family.[28] His having left Kufah, due to this event, is sufficient evidence that this distinct account was an indication towards the dangerous events of the future. In these very days, another disorder began to emerge as well.

'Abdullāh bin Sabā, was a Jew, also known as Ibnus-Saudā' on account of his mother.[29] He was a resident of Yemen and was an extremely evil person. Upon witnessing the growing success of Islam, he became a Muslim with the objective of somehow creating rift among the Muslims. In my view, it is this very mischievous person around whom the disorders of this era revolve, and who was in fact a driving force in this respect. It seems as if his inclination towards mischief was ingrained in his very nature. It was a habit for him to conspire secretly and

28. Tārīkhuṭ-Ṭabarī, vol. 5, p. 105, Dhikrus-Sababi Fī 'Azli....., Published by Dārul-Fikr, Beirut, 2002 edition [Publishers]
29. Tārīkhuṭ-Ṭabarī, vol. 5, p. 147, Dhikru Masīri Mann Sāra Ilā Dhī Khashabin Min Ahli Miṣra....., Published by Dārul-Fikr, Beirut, 2002 edition [Publishers]

he was highly skilled in identifying such people who could serve his motives. He would speak to everyone according to their dispositions and instigate vice in the veil of virtue. It is for this reason that even sincere people would fall victim to his deception. He became a Muslim in the first half of the *Khilāfat* of Ḥaḍrat 'Uthmān[ra] and toured all the Muslim States in order to personally gain insight as to the circumstances of each region. However, it was impossible for him to fulfil his ends in *Madīnah Munawwarah*.[30] At the time, Makkah was completely disconnected from politics. Apart from the capital – Basrah, Kufah, Damascus and Fustat were the political centres at the time. First he visited these places. He adopted a practice, whereby, he searched for such people who had been punished and were therefore displeased with the State. He would visit them and stay at their residence. First, he went to Basrah and stayed with Ḥakīm bin Jabalah, a robber who was under house arrest. He began to gather people of his own mentality and formed a party. As this was only the beginning of his mission and he was also a clever man, therefore, he would not speak openly; rather, he would call people towards mischief through subtle indications. Moreover, as was his ,long-standing custom, he continued his practice of admonition and exhortation as well. As a result of this, people began to develop reverence in their hearts for him and they began to accept his words. When 'Abdullāh bin 'Āmir, the governor of Basrah, came to know of this, he asked him how he was doing and enquired as to why he had come. At this, he sent a reply saying, *"I am a person from 'the*

30. Literally means, 'Madinah, the Enlightened' [Publishers]

People of the Book' who has fallen in love with Islam and wishes to stay under your protection." Since 'Abdullāh bin 'Āmir had already discovered the true state of affairs, he did not accept this plea and said, *"The information I possess about your state of affairs is in contradiction to what you claim, so leave my city."* Accordingly, he left Basrah and travelled towards Kufah.[31] However, before leaving, he managed to leave behind the seed of disorder and rebellion and aversion towards Islam.

In my opinion, this was the very first political error that took place. Instead of exiling him, if the governor of Basrah had imprisoned him and established a charge against him, perhaps this disorder may have remained there suppressed. The very intention behind Ibni Saudā' leaving his home was to inflame a fire of disorder and sedition by touring the whole of the Islamic Empire. His leaving Basrah was precisely in accordance with his objective. Upon reaching Kufah, he began to repeat the schemes he had undertaken in Basrah. Ultimately, he was exiled from here as well, but before moving on, he had managed to sow the seed of his mischief here as well, which later grew into very large tree. On this occasion, along with his exile, the political error that took place initially was committed once again. From Kufah he went to Syria, but was unable to find an opportunity to gain a foothold there. Here, Ḥaḍrat Mu'āwiyah[ra] was managing the affairs of State with such excellence that neither was Ibni Saudā' able to find such people amongst whom he could develop sway, nor could such people be found who could serve as his deputies.

---

31. Tārīkhuṭ-Ṭabarī, vol. 5, p. 139, Dhikrul-Khabari 'An Tasyīri 'Uthmān....., Published by Dārul-Fikr, Beirut, 2002 edition

Hence, he was forced to move on from Syria with regret and despair. Thus, he turned towards Egypt, but prior to leaving Syria he instigated another mischief.

Abū Dharr Ghifārī[ra] was an extremely pious and righteous man from among the pioneer Companions of the Holy Prophet[sa]. From the moment that he accepted Islam, his steps only advanced forward in the love of the Holy Prophet[sa]. He remained in the company of the Holy Prophet[sa] for a long period in time. Everyone possesses a unique disposition. Thus, upon hearing the admonition of the Holy Prophet[sa] that a believer should remain detached from the world, according to his own disposition, he viewed the accumulation of wealth as being unlawful and abhorred riches. He would also admonish others not to accumulate wealth and to distribute whatever they possessed amongst the poor. He had always held fast to this habit. Even in the era of Ḥaḍrat Abū Bakr, may Allah be pleased with him, when the Muslims became affluent, he held the same view. When Ibni Saudā' was passing through Syria, he noticed an extreme ebullience in his nature against wealth and his desire for the poor, as well as the rich, to distribute their wealth. Thus, upon travelling through Syria, he met with Ḥaḍrat Abū Dharr[ra], who resided there at the time, and said to him:

> *"Look at the injustice, Mu'āwiyah[ra] refers to the riches of baitul-māl[32] as being the wealth of Allah, although the funds of baitul-māl are not the only wealth that belongs to Allah; everything belongs to Allah the Exalted. Then why does he declare these funds to be the wealth of Allah*

32. National Treasury of the Islamic State [Publishers]

> *in particular? Only, so that he may usurp the right that Muslims have over these funds and after neglecting their share, so that he may devour this wealth himself."*

Ḥaḍrat Abū Dharr[ra] was already actively engaged in exhorting that the affluent should distribute all their wealth among the poor because the true abode of comfort for the beleivers is the hereafter. He was absolutely unaware of the mischief and motive of this person. As a result, he fell victim to his deception and actually began to think, that it was wrong to refer to the funds of *baitul-māl* as being the wealth of Allah, because there was a danger of the usurpation of wealth. In this manner, Ibni Saudā' took revenge from Ḥaḍrat Mu'āwiyah[ra] for not affording him an opportunity to develop a stronghold in Syria. Ḥaḍrat Abū Dharr[ra] went to Mu'āwiyah[ra] and admonished him, *"You refer to the wealth of Muslims, as being the wealth of Allah!"* To this, he replied:

> *"O Abū Dharr! May Allah the Exalted have mercy on you, are we not all the servants of Allah? Is this wealth not the wealth of Allah? Is all creation not the creation of Allah the Exalted? Is true authority not in the hands of God?"*

In other words, when the servants belong to God and it is His authority which reigns supreme then how would the rights of people be neglected by calling this wealth, the wealth of Allah? The rights which God the Exalted has fixed shall be given to His creation according to His command. This reply was so profound that Ḥaḍrat Abū Dharr[ra] was completely speechless. However, since he possessed special fervour in this regard and Ibni Saudā had planted a doubt in his heart, out of caution, he advised

Ḥaḍrat Mu'āwiyah[ra] to refrain from using this term. Ḥaḍrat Mu'āwiyah[ra] replied:

> *"I shall never say that these funds are not the wealth of Allah, but from now on, I shall refer to them as the wealth of the Muslims."*

When Ibni Saudā' found this tactic to prove somewhat effective, he approached other companions and tried to provoke them. However, they were reclusive in nature like Ḥaḍrat Abū Dharr[ra]. They were aware of this person's mischief. As soon as Abū Dardā'[ra] heard his words, he said, *"Who are you to say such seditious things? By God, you are a Jew!"* Left disappointed by such, he approached the chief of the *anṣār*,[33] 'Ubādah bin Ṣāmit[ra], an intimate Companion of the Holy Prophet[sa], and made certain mischievous statements. He apprehended him, took him to Ḥaḍrat Mu'āwiyah[ra] and said, *"This is the man who sent Abū Dharr Ghifārī[ra] to you."* When Ibni Saudā' was confronted with failure in Syria, he left for Egypt, but his words ignited a new zeal in Ḥaḍrat Abū Dharr[ra]. He began to admonish the Muslims with even greater passion than before that all of them should distribute their wealth amongst the people. It was not correct for Ḥaḍrat Abū Dharr[ra] to assert that no one should accumulate wealth. The reason being that the companions never hoarded wealth, rather, they always distributed their wealth in the cause of Allah. Invariably, they were definitely affluent, but this does not constitute the hoarding of wealth. The hoarding of wealth is only an applicable term when a person does not support the poor, and does not pay

33. A title of veneration given to the Muslims of Madinah [Publishers]

charity and alms. Even in the time of the Holy Prophet[sa] some of his companions were rich. If they had not been well-off, how could Ḥaḍrat 'Uthmān[ra] have afforded to provide ten thousand soldiers provisions of travel at the time of the *ghazwah*[34] of Tabūk. The Holy Prophet[sa] never reprimanded such people. In fact, some of them were very dear to the Holy Prophet[sa]. Hence, being affluent was no crime; instead, it was in direct accordance with the prophecies of the Holy Quran and Ḥaḍrat Abū Dharr, may Allah be pleased with him, was mistaken in this regard. However, whatever the case may have been, Ḥaḍrat Abū Dharr[ra] was adamant in respect of his own view. Nonetheless, it is also worthy of mention that although he would exhort people in light of his own view, he never took the law into his own hands. The commandments of the Holy Prophet[sa] forever remained under his consideration. However, the people in whose company he would sit and express these views were unacquainted with his virtue and piety and took his statements in a different light. Finally, the end result of these views was that certain poor people began to extend oppressive hands towards the affluent in an attempt to take their own rights from them by force. These people complained to Ḥaḍrat Mu'āwiyah[ra], who then submitted the matter before Ḥaḍrat 'Uthmān[ra]. Ḥaḍrat 'Uthmān[ra] issued an order for Ḥaḍrat Abū Dharr[ra] to be sent to Madinah with honour and dignity. As per this instruction, Ḥaḍrat Abū Dharr[ra] arrived in Madinah. Ḥaḍrat 'Uthmān[ra] inquired from him, *"Why do the people of Syria complain against you?"* He replied, *"I differ*

34. A military expedition in which the Holy Prophet[sa] took part himself. [Publishers]

with them because firstly, the term 'wealth of Allah' should not be used; secondly, the affluent should not accumulate wealth." Ḥaḍrat 'Uthmān[ra] explained:

> *"Abū Dharr[ra], it is my duty and mine alone to fulfil the responsibility that Allah the Exalted has laid upon me. It is also my obligation to enforce the subjects to discharge their responsibilities, to encourage them to serve religion and to be moderate. However, it is not my task to compel them to abandon the world."*

Ḥaḍrat Abū Dharr[ra] submitted, *"Then allow me to go somewhere else, because Madinah is no longer appropriate for me."* Ḥaḍrat 'Uthmān[ra] responded, *"Will you abandon this abode and adopt one that is inferior to this?"* He replied, *"The Holy Prophet[sa] told me that when the population of Madinah extends as far as Sal', do not stay in Madinah."* To this, Ḥaḍrat 'Uthmān, may Allah be pleased with him, responded, *"Then carry out the instruction of the Holy Prophet[sa]."* After giving him some camels and two slaves, Ḥaḍrat 'Uthmān[ra] bid him farewell, but stressed that he should not completely sever his ties with Madinah and continue visiting every so often. Abū Dharr[ra] always acted upon this guidance.[35] This was the fourth conflict which arose. Although Ḥaḍrat Abū Dharr[ra] was used as an instrument, the fact of the matter is that neither did he hold the same views as the rebels, nor was he aware of their mischief. Despite a difference of opinion, Ḥaḍrat Abū Dharr[ra] never set out to take the law into his own hands. He continued to obey the government to such an extent that in

35. Tārīkhuṭ-Ṭabarī, vol. 5, pp. 112-113, Akhbāru Abī Dharrin[ra]....., Published by Dārul-Fikr, Beirut, 2002 edition

consideration of his special circumstances, even though the Holy Prophet[sa] had instructed him to leave Madinah at a certain time in order to save him from trial and suffering, he did not deem it appropriate to even act upon this command without first seeking permission from Ḥaḍrat 'Uthmān[ra]. Moreover, when he left Madinah and settled in Rabdhah and the local tax collector asked him to become the Imām in congregational prayer, he refused saying, *"You are the governor here, thus, it is you who is best suited for being the Imām."* This demonstrates that he had no objection in being obedient to governors, nor did he view anarchy as being permissible.

The simplicity of Ḥaḍrat Abū Dharr[ra] becomes clearly evident from the fact that even after being deceived by Ibnus-Saudā', when he would argue with Mu'āwiyah[ra], that the funds of *baitul-māl* should not be called the wealth of Allah and even after submitting a complaint to Ḥaḍrat 'Uthmān[ra] as well, he constantly continued to use the same term in his own speech. Once, after this conflict, when he was in Rabdhah a caravan arrived. The people of the caravan enquired from him, *"We have seen your companions and they are incredibly affluent, but why are you living in such a state of poverty?"* He gave them the following response:

إِنَّهُمْ لَيْسَ لَهُمْ فِيْ مَالِ اللّٰهِ حَقٌّ إِلَّا وَلِيْ مِثْلُهُ

"They possess no right over the wealth of Allah, (i.e. the funds of baitul-māl) which I also do not possess."[36]

---

36. Tārīkhuṭ-Ṭabarī, vol. 5, p. 114, Akhbāru Abī Dharrin[ra]....., Published by Dārul-Fikr, Beirut, 2002 edition

Similarly he would also refer to the Abyssinian governor of that area as:

رَقِيْقٌ مِّنْ مَّالِ اللّٰهِ

"A servant of the wealth of Allah."[37]

This demonstrates that he would use this term himself as well. Furthermore, the fact that he could not help but uttering this phrase again and again testifies to the fact that this was a general figure of speech among the companions. However, Ḥaḍrat Abū Dharr[ra] forgot this due to the deception of Ibnus-Saudā'.

This disorder, which is best described as a Bolshevik conflict, could not succeed in Syria due to the strategic planning of Ḥaḍrat Mu'āwiyah[ra]. Nevertheless, in different forms, this view managed to spread in other regions and served as an aid in the work of Ibnus-Saudā'.

Ibnus-Saudā' left from Syria and arrived in Egypt. This was the place that chose to make the centre of his scheme because it was very far from the capital. Secondly, the companions did not visit it as often as other areas. For this reason, the local people were comparatively less familiar with religion and more willing to take part in conflict. The deputy of Ibnus-Saudā', who was a resident of Kufah and shall be mentioned later on, was exiled a short period after these events. When asked, in reply to the enquiry of Ḥaḍrat Mu'āwiyah[ra] as to the state of the members of this new party in different countries, he said:

---

37. Tārīkhuṭ-Ṭabarī, vol. 5, p. 114, Akhbāru Abī Dharrin[ra]....., Published by Dārul-Fikr, Beirut, 2002 edition

> *"I have been in correspondence with them, and it was I who guided them, not they. The people of Madinah are the keenest in creating disorder, but they are the least capable. The people of Kufah raise objections on trivial matters, but they are not afraid of committing grave sins. The people of Basrah attack together, but scatter when they flee. No doubt, it is the people of Egypt who are the most fit for mischief, but their shortcoming is that they become regretful soon after."*

After this, describing the situation of Syria he said, *"They are the most obedient to their chiefs and most disobedient to those who mislead them."*[38] This is the opinion of Ibnul-Kawwā' who was a member of the party of Ibnus-Saudā'. This establishes that Egypt was the most suitable place where Ibnus-Saudā' could setup camp. When his shrewd eye of mischief caught sight of this, he selected this as his place of residence and made it a centre of disorder. It was no time before a party had gathered around him.

Now, headquarters of mischief had been established in every city. With great skill and intelligence, Ibnus-Saudā' began to recruit such people who had either been sentenced, were relatives of such people, or were not content with their condition for one reason or another. He would express his view to such people according to their respective dispositions in order to gain their sympathy. Madinah was safe from mischief and Syria was completely free from it as well. There were three

38. * As shall be proven ahead, he lied when stating that the people of Madinah were not at all involved in this disorder.
* Tārīkhuṭ-Ṭabarī, vol. 5, p. 140, Dhikru Mā Kāna Minal-Aḥdāthi....., Published by Dārul-Fikr, Beirut, 2002 edition [Publishers]

centres where the material for conflict was being prepared, i.e. Basrah, Kufah and Egypt. Egypt was the headquarters. However, Ibnus-Saudā' had kept himself hidden behind veils, just like the experienced and philosophically minded anarchists of that era. He was the spirit behind this entire scheme but others had been pushed to the forefront. Due to being nearby and on account of the political superiority which Basrah and Kufah enjoyed at the time, the people of these two cities appear to be at the forefront of this revolution. However, if one looks closely, the pages of history clearly indicate that the reins of all these schemes was in the hands of Ibnus-Saudā', who lived in Egypt.

I have already mentioned that a party of men robbed the house of 'Alī bin Ḥaisumān Al-Khazā'ī in Kufah and then killed him, after which these murderers were executed at the gate of the city. The fathers of these young men were extremely shocked by this and desired to seek revenge from Walīd bin 'Utbah, the governor of that region. They waited eagerly for an opportunity to seek revenge. These people became an excellent weapon for the rebels, and fully utilised them. In order to seek revenge from Walīd, they appointed spies so that they could find a shortcoming in Walīd and inform them. The spies had to report something, so, one day, they came and relayed that Walīd meets with a Muslim friend Abū Zubair, who was previously a Christian, and drinks alcohol. The rebels rose up and began to announce to the whole city that this was the state of their governor. The fervour of the masses is, after all, uncontrollable. Upon hearing this, a large party joined them and they all besieged the house of Walīd. There was no door as such and everyone recklessly entered through the mosque (the door to his house opened into the mosque) and Walīd only came to know of them when they were standing right before him. Upon seeing them, he became perplexed and quickly hid something away under the bed. They thought that they had caught the thief red handed and the secret had now been revealed. Without uttering a single word someone promptly slipped his hand under the bed and pulled out the object. When they caught sight of it, they noticed that it was a tray with the food of the governor of Kufah and a bunch of grapes placed on it, which the Governor had hidden only in the embarrassment that such a small quantity of food had been presented before the Governor of such a wealthy province. At this, all of these people were left confounded and they turned on their heels in utter shame. They began to reproach one another for committing such a grave crime and for having discarded the commandments of the shariah due to being deceived by a few mischievous people. In his embarrassment, Walid buried the matter and did not inform Ḥaḍrat 'Uthmān[ra] of this incident. However, ultimately, this mercy of his, which he expressed to undeserving people, proved to be seriously detrimental for him and also for his deputy after him. Instead of being moved by his mercy, the rebels felt even more humiliated and began to connive for the destruction of Walīd with even greater fervour than before. They went to Ḥaḍrat 'Uthmān[ra] as a delegation for the dismissal of Walīd. However, Ḥaḍrat 'Uthmān[ra] refused to dismiss the governor without crime. When these people returned they began to gather all such people who had been sentenced and collectively deliberated as to how, by hook or by crook, Walīd could be disgraced. Two people named Abū Zainab and Abu Muwarri', took it upon themselves to devise a scheme and actively began to sit in his gatherings. One day they found an opportunity when no one else was around and Walīd had gone to sleep in the men's section, which was partitioned from the ladies section only by a sheet. The both of them slowly removed his ring and ran towards Madinah claiming to have seen Walīd drunk. They asserted that the ring was proof of this and they had removed it, without him noticing, when he was in a state of intoxication. Ḥaḍrat 'Uthmān[ra] inquired, *"Did he drink alcohol in front of you?"* They did not dare respond in the affirmative, because if such had been the case, this would implicate that they too were involved with Walīd. Instead, they responded, *"We saw him vomit alcohol."* The ring was at hand as evidence and two witnesses were present. In addition, a few other mischievous people accompanied them as well in order to further strengthen their testimony and continued to furnish circumstantial testimony of the incident. Counsel was sought from the companions and it was decided that Walīd would be punished for the consumption of alcohol. He was summoned from Kufah to Madinah and lashed as a penalty for drinking. Although Walīd defended himself and informed Ḥaḍrat 'Uthmān[ra] of their mischief, but Ḥaḍrat 'Uthmān[ra] responded:

> *"According to the law of the shariah you must receive a punishment as per the testimony of these witnesses. Of course, a person who gives false testimony shall be punished by Allah the Exalted."*[39]

Walid was deposed on a false account, but according to the

39. Tārīkhuṭ-Ṭabarī, vol. 5, pp. 105-108, Dhikrus-Sababi Fī 'Azli....., Published by Dārul-Fikr, Beirut, 2002 edition

counsel of the companions, Ḥaḍrat 'Uthmān[ra] sentenced him. Since witnesses and circumstantial evidence was present against him, it was necessary for him to be punished according to the law of the shariah. Sa'īd bin Al-'Āṣ[ra] was made the governor of Kufah and sent in his place. When he went to Kufah and saw the state that prevailed there, he was shocked. The delinquents of society and those who were unfamiliar with religion had primarily taken control and the well-mannered had been subjugated and suppressed. He informed Ḥaḍrat 'Uthmān[ra] of the matter, who advised him to restore the respect and honour of those who had offered great sacrifices and came forth to fight the opponents in earlier times. If, however, they demonstrated a lack of interest in religion, then of course, he could replace them with those who were more pious.[40]

When this mischief had broken out in Kufah, Basrah was not at rest. Through Ḥakīm bin Jabalah, an agent of Ibnus-Saudā', and his accomplices, false allegations were being spread against the deputies of Ḥaḍrat 'Uthmān[ra] there as well.

In Egypt, which was the real headquarters, even greater havoc had been wreaked. Not only had 'Abdullāh bin Sabā instigated political insurgency in this region; rather, he was also ruining the religion of people. However, he did this in a manner that people who were ignorant of faith would consider him very sincere. As such, he would preach saying:

"It is strange that various Muslims hold the belief that the Masīḥ [Messiah], on whom be peace, would return

40. Tārīkhuṭ-Ṭabarī, vol. 5, p. 109, Dhikrus-Sababi Fī 'Azli....., Published by Dārul-Fikr, Beirut, 2002 edition [Publishers]

to the world again. Yet, they do not believe that the Holy Prophet[sa] would be raised again. However, Allah the Exalted states in the Holy Quran:

اِنَّ الَّذِیۡ فَرَضَ عَلَیۡکَ الۡقُرۡاٰنَ لَرَآدُّکَ اِلٰی مَعَادٍ ؕ

'He Who has made the teaching of the Quran binding on you will most surely bring you back to the place of return.'"[*41]

Many of his followers accepted this teaching of his and became convinced of the [physical] re-advent of the Holy Prophet[sa] on earth, despite the fact that the Holy Quran strongly rejects the return to earth of those who have passed away. However, it is possible that in order to honour the name of such a person, Allah the Exalted raises some else after having endowed him the morals and attributes of that person. However, this concept is at complete odds with the belief of reincarnation or the return of a person [to earth]; this is an obvious and clear fact. In addition to this belief of *raj'at*, 'Abdullāh bin Sabā began to preach that thousands of prophets had passed and every prophet possessed a *waṣī*;[42] thus, the *waṣī* of the Holy Prophet[sa] was Ḥaḍrat 'Ali[ra]. If the Holy Prophet[sa] was *khātamul-anbiyā*'[43] then Ḥaḍrat 'Ali[ra] was *khātamul-auṣiyā'*. Then he would say, *"Who can be more*

41. * This prophecy was actually about the victory of Makkah, which was distorted by him in order to concoct the belief of *raj'at*. Since people travel to Makkah again and again for the purpose of hajj and to attain spiritual reward, this is why it is also called *ma'ād* i.e., a place where people return often.
 * Al-Qaṣaṣ (28:86)
42. See glossary of terms for further details [Publishers]
43. Seal of the Prophets [Publishers]

unjust than a person who attacks the waṣī of the Holy Prophet[sa] *and snatches his right?"*[44]

Therefore, aside from the political strategies that this person employed in order to create rift in Islam, he had instigated a religious disorder as well. Furthermore, he was also conniving to corrupt the beliefs of Muslims, but took precautions to ensure that people considered him to be a Muslim.

In this state of affairs, three years elapsed and this mischievous group continued to carry out these secret conspiracies. This party continued to multiply in number. However, in this three year period no significant incident transpired except that two residents of *Madīnah Munawwarah* named Muḥammad bin Abī Bakr and Muḥammad bin Abī Ḥudhaifah, began to take part in this disorder to some extent as well.[45] Muḥammad bin Abī Bakr was the younger son of Ḥaḍrat Abū Bakr[ra] and except for the fact that he possessed the distinction of being the son of Ḥaḍrat Abū Bakr[ra], he held no religious merit. Muḥammad bin Abī Ḥudhaifah was an orphan who had been brought up by Ḥaḍrat 'Uthmān[ra]. However, after reaching an age of maturity, he played a prominent role in the uprising against Ḥaḍrat 'Uthmān[ra]. I shall explain why shortly hereafter. In the fourth year, this conflict took on somewhat

44. Tārīkhuṭ-Ṭabarī, vol. 5, p. 147, Dhikru Masīri Mann Sāra Ilā Dhī Khashabin Min Ahli Miṣra....., Published by Dārul-Fikr, Beirut, 2002 edition [Publishers]

45. Tārīkhuṭ-Ṭabarī, vol. 5, p.p 117-118, Dhikrul-Khabari 'An Maqtali Yazdajar....., Published by Dārul-Fikr, Beirut, 2002 edition [Publishers]

of a terrifying state and its originators thought that now it was appropriate to openly express their views and to wipe out the awe of the State. Consequently, in this regard as well, Kufah was first to advance.

As I have already mentioned, Sa'īd bin Al-'Āṣ[ra] was appointed governor of Kufah after Walīd bin 'Utbah. From the outset he had adopted the custom of only allowing noble townsmen to come into his company. However, at times, he would also hold an open gathering when men of all types would be allowed to come into his company. One day, they were sitting in such a gathering when the subject of the generosity of Ḥaḍrat Ṭalḥah[ra] came under discussion. Someone said that Ḥaḍrat Ṭalḥah[ra] always acted with extreme generosity. In response to this Sa'īd happened to utter the words:

> *"He possesses a great deal of wealth, and so he is charitable; if we also possessed such wealth, we too, would demonstrate such generosity and munificence."*

A young man naively said:

> *"If only such and such property, which once belonged to the royal treasury and had been kept for the benefit of ordinary Muslims, had been in your possession. "*

At this, a few men who belonged to the party of rebels and were waiting for an opportunity to arise so that they could express their views, began to express their anger. They asserted that the person had made this statement on the indication of Sa'īd, the governor of Kufah; so that a pathway could be paved in order to usurp this wealth. As such, they stood up and began to beat this person right before Sa'īd. When his father stood up to assist him, they thoroughly beat him as well. Sa'īd continuously attempted to restrain them but they did not even pay heed to him; and beat the two until they both fell unconscious. When the public received news that certain people had committed such an act of mischief in the very presence of Sa'īd, they gathered outside his house armed. However, the perpetrators begged and pleaded Sa'īd for forgiveness and asked for his refuge. How could the generosity of an Arab, and then a one from the Quraish, possibly bear to refuse the plea of an enemy for refuge at such an occasion. Sa'īd stepped out and said to the public, *"A few people fell to confrontation; the matter is of no significance and everything is now in order."* Everyone returned to their homes, and once again these people began to feel at ease. When Sa'īd was certain that the perpetrators were out of danger, he let them go. Then he addressed the people who had been beaten and said:

> *"As I have already given these people refuge, do not publicise their crime, or I shall be disgraced. Rest assured, however, that they shall not be allowed in my company again."*[46]

The rebels had already succeeded in their real objective i.e. to create disturbance in the Islamic administration. Now, they had began to openly criticise Ḥaḍrat 'Uthmān[ra] and Sa'īd in their homes. The public was greatly offended by this behaviour and complained to Sa'īd saying:

> *"These people are causing mischief in this manner. They criticise Ḥaḍrat 'Uthmān[ra] and you, and seek to uproot the unity of Islam. We cannot tolerate this; please resolve the matter."*

46. Tārīkhuṭ-Ṭabarī, vol. 5, pp. 133-134, Dhikru Tasyīri Mann Sayyara Min Ahlil-Kūfata Ilaihā, Published by Dārul-Fikr, Beirut, 2002 edition [Publishers]

He replied, *"Inform Ḥaḍrat 'Uthmān*[ra] *of all the events yourself and the matter shall be dealt with in accordance with his instructions."* All the noble people informed Ḥaḍrat 'Uthmān[ra] of the events, who ordered Sa'īd that if the leaders of Kufah unanimously agreed, these people should be exiled towards Syria and sent to Amir Mu'āwiyah. Then, he wrote to Amir Mu'āwiyah[ra] saying:

> *"A few people, who are openly bent upon creating disorder, shall come to you from Kufah. Make preparations for their subsistence and devise a plan for their reform. If they improve and reform themselves, then treat them with compassion and overlook their faults, but if they persist in mischief then punish them."*[47]

This order of Ḥaḍrat 'Uthmān[ra] was based on immense wisdom because on the one hand, their living in Kufah would provoke the public's anger, who was fully aware of their mischief; and there was a danger of them being incited and causing them harm; on the other hand, it was also injurious because these people were residents there and possessed a degree of influence. If they had continued to live there, they would have become a means for misguiding many others.[48] However, this verdict was issued at a time when much benefit could not be expected. If Ibni 'Āmir, the governor of Basrah, had also sought advice

47. Tārīkhuṭ-Ṭabarī, vol. 5, p. 134, Dhikru Tasyīri Mann Sayyara Min Ahlil-Kūfat Ilaihā, Published by Dārul-Fikr, Beirut, 2002 edition [Publishers]

48. They were unable to find an opportunity to mislead people in the place where they were exiled because they were kept under special supervision and strict watch.

from Ḥaḍrat 'Uthmān[ra] regarding Ibnus-Saudā' and a similar instruction had been given for him, perhaps latter events may have turned out differently. However, the state of the Muslims at the time demanded that such should be its fate and destiny; and so it occurred.

These people who were exiled and should best be referred to as members of the party of Ibni Sabā, were close to ten in number (although there is a disagreement in their actual number). The first strategy that Ḥaḍrat Mu'āwiyah[ra] adopted for their reformation was to treat them with great honour and reverence. He would eat with them and often go and sit in their company, during his leisure time. After a few days, he advised them saying:

> *"I have heard that you hold enmity for the Quraish,[49] while this should not be the case. It is through the Quraish that Allah the Exalted has endowed glory to the Arabs. Your governors are like your shields so do not part from these shields, for they bear hardships on your account and are concerned for you. If you do not value this, God the Exalted shall appoint such rulers upon you who shall oppress you severely; shall not value your patience and a*

49. It is clearly evident from the statement of Ḥaḍrat Mu'āwiyah and the reply of these people that they were not opposed to Ḥaḍrat 'Uthmān[ra] or his appointed Governors. They opposed the Quraish; in other words, they harboured jealousy against those who were the foremost in belief. If a companion other than Ḥaḍrat 'Uthmān[ra] had been *Khalīfah*, and other Governors had been appointed in place of those who already held office, these people would have held enmity towards them in the same manner, because their only objective was to attain grandeur.

punishment shall befall you in this very world. Then, in the hereafter you shall be punished along with these tyrant rulers for their oppression, because it was you who became the means for their having assumed power."

Upon hearing this admonition of Ḥaḍrat Mu'āwiyah[ra] one of them replied:

"Do not speak of the Quraish, neither were they greater than us in number before, nor are they greater now; and as for the shield you speak of - if it is snatched - it is we who shall receive it."

Ḥaḍrat Mu'āwiyah[ra] said:

"It appears that you are foolish as well. I speak to you about the teachings of Islam and you remind me of the era of jāhiliyyah.[50] The question is not of the minority or majority of the Quraish, but of the responsibility Islam has laid upon them. No doubt, the Quraish are few, but when God the Exalted has honoured them with the religion of Islam and has continued to protect them since time immemorial due to their connection with Makkah, then who can compete with the bounty of God. When they were disbelievers, He protected them due to this insignificant connection. Now, after accepting Islam they have become the upholders of His religion. Would then God the Exalted waste them now? Keep in mind that you became Muslims along with the crowd, upon witnessing the victory of Islam. Now, Satan is using you as a weapon in order to destroy

50. Literally means 'ignorance,' and refers to the pre-Islamic era. [Publishers]

Islam and desires to create rift in religion. However, Allah the Exalted shall cast you into a greater trial than the one you desire to create. In my opinion, you are not the least worthy of any attention. The people who wrote to the Khalīfah with regards to you, committed a mistake. Neither can any benefit be expected of you, nor harm."

Upon listening to all of the advice of Ḥaḍrat Mu'āwiyah[ra], these people said, *"We order you to step down from your office."* Ḥaḍrat Mu'āwiyah[ra] replied:

"If the Khalīfah and the Muslim leaders ask me to, then I shall resign from office today. Who are you to interfere in these matters. I advise you to mend your ways and to adopt piety. Allah the Exalted does His work Himself. If matters were decided in accordance to your wishes, then the work of Islam would come to ruin. In actuality, you are averse to the very religion of Islam. In your hearts is one thing and upon your tongues is quite the opposite. However, one day, Allah the Exalted shall certainly disclose your intentions and secret schemes."

As such, Ḥaḍrat Mu'āwiyah[ra] spent a great deal of time advising them, but they only continued to move further in their disrespect. Ultimately, when they were left speechless, they attacked Ḥaḍrat Mu'āwiyah[ra] in an attempt to kill him but Ḥaḍrat Mu'āwiyah[ra] scolded them saying:

"This is Syria, not Kufah. If the Syrians learn of this, they shall not remain silent as the people of Kufah did upon the request of Sa'īd. In their vehemence, the masses shall not even listen to me and tear you to pieces."

Having said this, Ḥaḍrat Mu'āwiyah[ra] left the gathering and sent them back to Kufah. He then wrote to Ḥaḍrat 'Uthmān[ra]:

> *"These people are not the least worthy of attention due to their foolishness and ignorance. We should not give them any attention. It should also be written to Sa'īd, the governor of Kufah, not to pay any attention to them. They are irreligious people and averse to Islam. They desire to rob the wealth of those in a position of responsibility and have the habit of creating disorder. They do not have the strength to cause harm themselves without the aid of others."*[51]

The opinion of Ḥaḍrat Mu'āwiyah[ra] was absolutely correct but he was unaware that there was a soul hiding outside his territory, in Egypt, who was using all of them; and his cause was best served by their ignorance and foolishness.

When these people left Damascus, they abandoned their plan of going to Kufah, since the people who lived there were already familiar with their mischief. They also feared that they would suffer harm there; hence they went towards Jazīrah. The governor of this region, 'Abdur-Raḥmān, was the pious son of the renowned general who had left behind a shining legacy of courage and bravery for the whole world, i.e., Khālid bin Walīd. When he learnt of their arrival, he immediately called for them and said:

> *"I have heard of your state of affairs. May Allah ruin me if I am unable to reform you. You are aware that I am*

51. Tārīkhuṭ-Ṭabarī, vol. 5, pp. 134-135/138, Dhikru Tasyīri Mann Sayyara Min Ahlil-Kūfat Ilaihā, Published by Dārul-Fikr, Beirut, 2002 edition [Publishers]

> *the son of that man who removed the disorder of apostasy and emerged victorious from great difficulties. I shall see whether you are able to talk to me in the manner that you spoke to Mu'āwiyah*[ra] *and Sa'īd*[ra]*. Listen here! If you utter a word of mischief to someone here, then I shall give you a punishment that you will never forget."*

Having said this, he confined them and ordered them to always remain with him. When he would go on journey, he would take them along with him on foot and he would inquire:

> *"How do you feel now? Punishment is the remedy of a person who is not reformed by virtue. Why do you not speak now?"*

These people would express remorse and seek repentance for their mischief. After some time had elapsed, 'Abdur-Raḥmān bin Khālid bin Walīd thought that they had been reformed. As such, he sent a person from among them by the name of Mālik to Ḥaḍrat 'Uthmān[ra] in order to beg for forgiveness. He came before Ḥaḍrat 'Uthmān[ra] and repented and expressed remorse and asked forgiveness for himself and his companions. Ḥaḍrat 'Uthmān[ra] forgave him and inquired as to where he desired to live. Mālik replied that now he wished to stay with 'Abdur-Raḥmān bin Khālid. Ḥaḍrat 'Uthmān[ra] granted him permission and he returned to 'Abdur-Raḥmān bin Khālid.[52]

His desire to stay with 'Abdur-Raḥmān bin Khālid indicates that his heart had certainly been cleansed at the time. If not, he would not have desired to return to such a man, who

52. Tārīkhuṭ-Ṭabarī, vol. 5, pp. 135-136, Dhikru Tasyīri Mann Sayyara Min Ahlil-Kūfata Ilaihā, Published by Dārul-Fikr, Beirut, 2002 edition [Publishers]

would not tolerate mischief for even a minute. However, later events substantiate that his repentance was only temporary and the opinion of Ḥaḍrat Mu'āwiyah[ra] was correct, in that these were foolish people who were only good for being used as weapons.

In the meanwhile, 'Abdullāh bin Sabā had not remained idle. Quite the contrary, for some time, he had adopted the strategy of dispatching agents to various regions and thus, spread his views. Without a shadow of doubt, this was a man of extraordinary intelligence and judgement. The orders he would give to his agents shed ample light on the framework of his mind. Whilst dispatching his representatives, he would advise them:

> *"Do not be hasty in disclosing your views to people at once; rather, exhort and advise them first. Recite to them the injunctions of the shariah. Enjoin goodness and forbid evil. When the people observe this manner of admonition, their hearts will be drawn towards you. They will listen to you with enthusiasm and will begin to trust you. Only then present your particular views skilfully; they will accept them very quickly. Moreover, be cautious not to speak against Ḥaḍrat 'Uthmān[ra] at the very outset; rather, incite people against his representatives first."*

The purpose behind this was that since the people held a special religious attachment with Ḥaḍrat 'Uthmān[ra], they would become enraged upon hearing words against him. However, they would accept statements against governors as this would not move their religious sentiments. In this manner, when their hearts would turn black and the obstinacy that results from joining a certain party would develop, then it would also become easier to incite them against Ḥaḍrat 'Uthmān[ra].

This person realised that whenever the shortcomings of provincial governors were mentioned, the wise would refuse to accept them, because these people knew that they were false and unfounded based on their own observation; and widespread uproar would not arise throughout the country. Therefore, he undertook another dangerous scheme. Instead of defaming the governors of various regions in their own jurisdictions, he ordered his representatives to write the failings of governors to other provinces, because the people of other regions would easily accept such statements due to their unfamiliarity with the circumstances of that area. According to this proposal, the rebels of all the various regions would write false complaints and cruelties of their local governors to the sympathetic people of other towns. These people would then read such letters to others and many of them would be convinced of their truth due to being unaware of the circumstances in foreign lands. They would feel grieved at the thought that their brethren were afflicted by extreme difficulties in such and such land. At the same time, they would also be grateful that by the grace of Allah their own governors were kind and they were at ease. However, they were unaware that the people in other provinces believed themselves to be in a state of comfort and others in difficulty, and they were thankful for their own condition and felt concern for the state of others. Since the people of Madinah were receiving correspondence from all four fronts, those among them who considered these letters as being true would think that perhaps atrocities were being perpetrated in every province and hardships were befalling the Muslims. Hence, the deception of 'Abdullāh bin Sabā proved to be very effective and by this means he managed to gain thousands of sympathetic people who would have been difficult to find without such a scheme.

When this disturbance exceeded all bounds and even the noble companions began to receive letters of complaint against governors, together, they approached Ḥaḍrat 'Uthmān[ra] and submitted, *"Are you not aware of what is taking place outside Madinah?"* Ḥaḍrat 'Uthmān[ra] replied, *"The reports that I receive indicate nothing but peace and tranquility."* The companions responded that they were receiving letters of such and such subject matter, and this should be investigated. At this, Ḥaḍrat 'Uthmān[ra] sought their counsel as to how the investigation should be carried out. According to their proposal Usāmah bin Zaid[ra] was sent to Basrah, Muḥammad bin Maslamah to Kufah, 'Abdullāh bin 'Umar to Syria and 'Ammār bin Yāsir to Egypt, in order to investigate the state of affairs and report whether the governors were actually treating the citizens unjustly, oppressing them and usurping the rights of people. In addition to these four, he also dispatched some others to various lands so that they could provide a report of the conditions there.[53]

These people went and returned after having performed their investigation and all of them reported that it was peaceful everywhere and that Muslims were living their lives in complete freedom; no one was infringing upon their rights and the governors were acting with equity and justice. However,

53. Tārīkhuṭ-Ṭabarī, vol. 5, pp. 147-148, Dhikru Masīri Mann Sāra Ilā Dhī Khashabin Min Ahli Miṣra....., Published by Dārul-Fikr, Beirut, 2002 edition

'Ammār bin Yāsir was delayed and no news came from him.[54] I will mention why 'Ammār bin Yāsir was delayed later on, but first I would like to mention something about this investigative committee and the significance of this investigation. The reason being that the true reality of this disorder becomes clearly evident by fully understanding the specifics of this delegation. The first thing that is worthy of attention, is the stature of the three leading members of this delegation who returned to submit their reports. The status of the people carrying out this investigation demonstrates the significance of the investigation. If such people had been dispatched as part of this delegation, who desired something from Ḥaḍrat 'Uthmān[ra] and his deputies, or who, on account of their low and insignificant spiritual and worldly status may have feared the governors or harboured greed, it could be suggested that these people refrained from disclosing the truth on account of their greed or fear. However, such an allegation cannot be levelled against them. Furthermore, by selecting these people to perform this task, Ḥaḍrat 'Uthmān[ra] has furnished clear evidence of his pure intention. Usāmah[ra], the one sent to Bashrah, was not only the son of Ḥaḍrat Zaid[ra], who was first among those who believed, but was also from among the closest and dearest ones of the Holy Prophet[sa]. He was the very person upon whom the Holy Prophet[sa] conferred the position of being commander-in-chief of the magnificent army that he was prepared during his final illness. He also positioned eminent companions like Ḥaḍrat 'Umar[ra] in subordination

54. Tārīkhuṭ-Ṭabarī, vol. 5, p. 148, Dhikru Masīri Mann Sāra Ilā Dhī Khashabin Min Ahli Miṣra....., Published by Dārul-Fikr, Beirut, 2002 edition [Publishers]

to him. This selection by the Holy Prophet[sa] was not merely an act of encouragement. In fact, later events established that he was capable of achieving great feats. The Holy Prophet[sa] displayed so much love for him that spectators would be unable to differentiate whether he loved him more or Ḥaḍrat Imām Ḥasan[ra]. Muḥammad bin Muslim, who was sent to Kufah, was also from among the most venerable companions. He was looked upon with great reverence amongst the companions and was very influential.

'Abdullāh bin 'Umar[ra], who was sent to Syria, is among those who require no introduction. He was among the foremost Muslims who pledged their allegiance. He was so great in his piety and righteousness that on account of this particular merit, even the most prominent companions displayed a special respect for him. After Ḥaḍrat 'Ali[ra] if the sight of the companions and other noble men fell upon anyone for succession to *Khilāfat*, then it was him. However, he had made it a practice to remain secluded from the world. He possessed such indignation for those things that were deemed sacred in religion that on certain occasions, he even vehemently debated 'Umar bin Al-Khaṭṭāb[ra]. Hence, in speaking the truth, he was an unsheathed sword. His appointment for Syria was a most perfect appointment. Ḥaḍrat Mu'āwiyah[ra] had long been the governor of Syria and held a position of great awe upon the residents there. Due to his intelligence, investigating his administration was not the task of an ordinary person. It was futile to send anyone else to this region and no one would have been satisfied with the investigation of such a person. However, his excellence in faith, indignation for Islam, farsightedness, righteousness and piety were such merits, before which even Mu'āwiyah[ra] could not dare to utter a word. In his presence the awe of Ḥaḍrat Mu'āwiyah[ra] could not influence anyone.

Therefore, the people who were sent to carry out this investigation were magnificent and neutral people and no one can raise an objection against their findings. The unanimous verdict of these three companions along with the rest of those who were sent to other countries that there was absolute peace and security, no sign of injustice and tyranny, and governors were acting with complete equality and justice; and if they were liable to be blamed then it was only inasmuch that they compelled people to remain within boundaries, was such a verdict which leaves no room for doubt. It is clearly evident that all this disorder was the result of the mischief of a few transgressors and the instigation of 'Abdullāh bin Sabā. Ḥaḍrat 'Uthmān[ra] and his representatives were free from all objections.

In truth, this entire disturbance was the result of a secret conspiracy hatched by the Jews. They were joined by certain Muslims who were attracted to the desire of the world and had left their faith. Neither were the provincial governors to blame for this, nor were they the cause of this disorder. Their only fault was that they had been appointed by Ḥaḍrat 'Uthmān[ra] and the fault of Ḥaḍrat 'Uthmān[ra] was that he was holding fast to the rope of Islamic unity despite his old age and physical weakness. He was carrying the burden of the Muslim ummah upon his shoulders and was concerned for the establishment of the Islamic shariah. He would not allow the rebellious and tyrannous to oppress the weak and helpless according to their desire. As such, the following incident testifies to the truth of this fact. When the same rebels held a meeting in Kufah and they began to discuss how disorder may be created in Muslim affairs, everyone unanimously gave the opinion:

وَ اللّٰهِ لَا يَرْفَعُ رَأسٌ مَا دَامَ عُثْمَانُ عَلَى النَّاسِ

"By God, no one can dare to raise their head, so long as the reign of 'Uthmān[ra] prevails."

It was the very person of Ḥaḍrat 'Uthmān[ra] himself which prevented rebellion. It was necessary to move him aside in order for these people to freely achieve their goals.[55]

Earlier, I explained that 'Ammār bin Yāsir, who had been sent to Egypt, did not return. There was a delay in receiving news from him to such extent that the residents of Madinah thought that he may have been killed. However, the fact of the matter was that due to his simplicity and unfamiliarity with politics, he had fallen into the clutches of the rebels, who were disciples of 'Abdullāh bin Sabā. As 'Abdullāh bin Sabā was present in Egypt himself, he was not oblivious to the fact that if this investigative committee reported a state of peace and security throughout the land, everyone would turn against them. The decision to send this delegation had been made so suddenly that he was unable to make arrangements in other provinces. However, it was easy for him to make arrangements in Egypt. He welcomed 'Ammār bin Yāsir as soon as he arrived in Egypt and began to describe the weaknesses and cruelties of the governor of Egypt. 'Ammār bin Yāsir was unable to safeguard himself from the enchantment of

55. Tārīkhuṭ-Ṭabarī, vol. 5, p. 189, Dhikru Ba'di Siyari 'Uthmānibni 'Affāna, Published by Dārul-Fikr, Beirut, 2002 edition [Publishers]

his words. Instead of carrying out an unbiased investigation, he did not even approach the governor of Egypt, nor did he carry out an ordinary investigation. On the contrary, he went along with this group of rebels and began to raise objections with them.[56]

'Ammār bin Yāsir is the only person from among the companions about whom it is categorically proven that he became entrapped in the snare of rebels. Aside from him, no other prominent Companion participated in such an act. If anyone from among them has been implicated, such a notion has been refuted by other narrations. There was a particular reason for 'Ammār bin Yāsir[ra] being deceived. As soon as he arrived in Egypt, he happened to meet a group of eloquent and well-spoken people who appeared to be reliable; they began to complain to him about the governor of Egypt with great skill. Coincidently, the governor of Egypt was a man who had once been a bitter enemy of the Holy Prophet[sa]. At the victory of Makkah the Holy Prophet[sa] had commanded that he should be killed even if he was to be found in the vicinity of the Ka'bah. Even though the Holy Prophet[sa] later forgave him, his former opposition had left traces of dislike upon the hearts of certain companions, which included 'Ammār[ra]. Therefore, upon hearing complaints against such a person, 'Ammār[ra] was very quickly influenced and accepted all the allegations that would be levelled against him as being true. Whilst capitalising on natural sentiment, the Sabā'īs, i.e., the supporters of 'Abdullāh

56. Tārīkhuṭ-Ṭabarī, vol. 5, p. 148, Dhikru Masīri Mann Sāra Ilā Dhī Khashabin Min Ahli Miṣra....., Published by Dārul-Fikr, Beirut, 2002 edition [Publishers]

bin Sabā, would highlight this particular issue as a means against the governor. The goodness of intention and sincerity of Ḥaḍrat 'Uthmān[ra] may be gauged from the fact that despite all the delegations giving a verdict absolving the governors, Ḥaḍrat 'Uthmān[ra] valued this single view to such extent that he wrote a letter to all the various regions. The contents of this letter was:

> *"Ever since I have become the Khalīfah I have acted upon enjoining equity and forbidding evil and my relatives do not hold a superior right to ordinary Muslims. However, I have come to know from certain residents of Madinah that the governors beat people and hurl abuse at them. For this reason I make an open announcement by way of this letter that whomsoever has been sworn at or beaten in secrecy, should meet me in Makkah Mukarramah[57] on the occasion of hajj. In return for any injustice done by my hand or by my governors, retribution may be sought from me and my representatives, or if such a person wills, he may forgive us. Allah the Exalted Himself rewards those who give ṣadaqah [i.e., those who forgive].*

When this brief but painful letter was read out upon the pulpits throughout the land, the Muslim world was shook from end to end. Listeners helplessly burst into tears and everyone prayed for Ḥaḍrat 'Uthmān[ra]. Everyone expressed displeasure towards these transgressors who were attacking and causing grief to a man who held sympathy for the Muslim ummah and carried its burden.[58]

57. Literally means, 'Makkah, the Honoured.' [Publishers]
58. Tārīkhuṭ-Ṭabarī, vol. 5, p. 148, Dhikru Masīri Mann Sāra Ilā Dhī Khashabin Min Ahli Miṣra....., Published by Dārul-Fikr, Beirut, 2002 edition

Ḥaḍrat 'Uthmān[ra] did not cease at this; he especially summoned his governors in order to answer for the allegations which had been levelled against them. When all of the governors had come together, he inquired of them, *"What is the reason for these allegations being levelled against you? I fear that they may be true."*

In response to this, they all submitted:

> *"You have sent reliable people and discovered that no injustice is being perpetrated, nor is anything being committed in violation of the shariah. Furthermore, the reliable people you dispatched inquired of the state of affairs from all the people. Not a single person came before them and claimed that these complaints were valid. What room, then, is there for doubt? By God, these people have not spoken the truth nor have they acted with the fear of Allah. Their allegations have no foundation. It cannot be permissible to hold one accountable for such baseless things, nor can such statements be relied upon."*

Ḥaḍrat 'Uthmān[ra] responded, *"Then suggest as to what should be done."* At this, many suggestions were given to him. In summary, it was suggested that Ḥaḍrat 'Uthmān[ra] should act sternly when the occasion demanded and not show leniency towards these mischief-makers, for this only increases them in fearlessness; an evil person can only be reformed through punishment, leniency should only be exhibited towards such a person who derives benefit from it. After listening to suggestions of everyone, Ḥaḍrat 'Uthmān[ra] said:

> *"The disorders which the Holy Prophet[sa] has informed us about are bound to take place, but they can be deferred*

for some time through gentleness and love. Therefore, except in the case of apparent violations of the law, I will treat them with leniency so that no one may hold a valid objection against me. Allah the Exalted knows that I have not been miserly in showing kindness to people. It would be joyous if 'Uthmān were to die and the flood of disorders, which are soon to overcome Islam, had not yet surged forth. Go, therefore, and treat people with compassion; give them their rights and overlook their faults. Of course, if someone violates the injunctions of Allah the Exalted, then do not show leniency and forgiveness to such people."[59]

On the return from hajj, Ḥaḍrat Mu'āwiyah[ra] also accompanied Ḥaḍrat 'Uthmān[ra] to Madinah. After having stayed there for a few days, when he was about to depart, he met Ḥaḍrat 'Uthmān[ra] in privacy and said, *"It appears that disorder is growing, if you permit, may I submit something in this regard?"* Ḥaḍrat 'Uthmān[ra] said, *"Go on."* Upon this, he said:

"My first proposal is that you accompany me to Syria as it is peaceful there in every respect; there is no disorder whatsoever. I fear that if disorder suddenly arises we may not be able to make arrangements at the time."

Ḥaḍrat 'Uthmān[ra] replied, *"I cannot leave the neighbourhood of the Holy Prophet[sa] under any circumstance, even if my body is torn to pieces."* Ḥaḍrat Mu'āwiyah[ra] said:

"Then my second proposal is that you grant me permission

59. Tārīkhuṭ-Ṭabarī, vol. 5, pp. 148-149, Dhikru Masīri Mann Sāra Ilā Dhī Khashabin Min Ahli Miṣra....., Published by Dārul-Fikr, Beirut, 2002 dition [Publishers]

> *to send a contingent of the Syrian army for your protection. No one shall be able to make mischief in its presence."*

Ḥaḍrat 'Uthmānra replied:

> *"Neither can I burden baitul-māl to such extent in order to safeguard the life of 'Uthmān, nor can I tolerate putting the people of Madinah to difficulty by maintaining a military presence."*

Upon this, Ḥaḍrat Mu'āwiyahra submitted:

> *"Then my third proposal is that you send off the companions to various countries, because in their presence, people possess the courage to assume that if you do not remain, some else may be put forward in your stead."*

Ḥaḍrat 'Uthmānra replied, *"How is it possible for me to scatter those whom the Holy Prophetsa has gathered?"* Upon hearing this, Ḥaḍrat Mu'āwiyahra began to weep and submitted:

> *"If you do not accept any of these strategies which I have proposed for your protection then at least announce to the people, 'If any harm comes to me then Mu'āwiyah shall possess the right to retaliate on my behalf.' Perhaps, people shall refrain from making mischief in fear on this account."*

Ḥaḍrat 'Uthmānra replied:

> *"Mu'āwiyah! What is to happen will surely come to pass. I cannot grant this permission since you possess a stern disposition and may treat the Muslims harshly."*

Thereupon, Ḥaḍrat Mu'āwiyahra stood up weeping and said, *"I fear this may be our last meeting."* When he stepped outside, he said to the companions, *"The fate of Islam rests upon you. Ḥaḍrat*

'Uthman[ra] has now fallen very weak. Disorder is escalating. Please do look after him."[60]

After saying this, Mu'āwiyah[ra] set off for Syria.

The absence of provincial governors from their respective regions, was not an opportunity that 'Abdullāh bin Sabā would simply allow to slip away. He immediately relayed a message in all directions saying:

> *"Now is the perfect time for us to act. Let us choose one day and launch a sudden attack upon the governors of our respective provinces."*

However, they were still consulting one other when the governors happened to return. The Sabā'īs (i.e. supporters of 'Abdullāh bin Sabā) in other areas were left in despair, but as for those in Kufah, who were already habitual in being at the forefront of practical disorder, did not let this opportunity slip away. A person by the name of Yazīd bin Qais held a gathering in the Kufah mosque and announced that Ḥaḍrat 'Uthmān[ra] should now be removed from the office of *Khilāfat*. When Qa'qā' bin 'Amr[ra], who was the officer of the military post there, heard of this, he came to arrest him. Yazīd bin Qais made a plea before him stating:

> *"I am not acting disobediently. We have only gathered to hold a meeting about Sa'īd bin Al-'Āṣ[ra] so that we can request his return from here and the appointment of a new officer in his stead."*

The officer replied:

---

60. Tārīkhuṭ-Ṭabarī, vol. 5, p. 150, Dhikru Masīri Mann Sāra Ilā Dhī Khashabin Min Ahli Miṣra....., Published by Dārul-Fikr, Beirut, 2002 edition [Publishers]

> *"There is no need to hold gatherings for this purpose. Write your complaints and send them to Ḥaḍrat 'Uthmān[ra]. He will appoint another governor and send him here. What is the difficulty in this?"*

The reason he said this was because in the time of the *Khulafā',* whenever a complaint would arise against governors, in most cases, they would be replaced out of a concern for the welfare of people. Upon hearing this reply of Qa'qā', they seemingly dispersed, but continued to conspire in secret. Ultimately, Yazīd bin Qais, who was the leader of the Sabā'īs in Kufah at the time, sent someone with a letter to Homs and told him to bring back those who had been exiled from Kufah and whose incident has been mentioned earlier. The subject matter of this letter was that the people of Egypt have joined us; as soon as you receive this letter return immediately, without a moments delay.[61]

How ironic is it that the people who were demonstrating rage and raising allegations against the *Khalīfah* of the time - the foremost in faith and the son-in-law of the Holy Prophet[sa] - were those who had themselves abandoned the obligatory prayers. Is it possible that indignation for Islam should only manifest itself within the faithless? If a shortcoming or something in contradiction with the shariah truly existed in Ḥaḍrat 'Uthmān[ra] or his governors, then the people who would have expressed their anger against this would have been 'Alī, Ṭalḥah, Zubair, Sa'd bin Waqqāṣ, 'Abdullāh bin 'Amr, Usāmah bin Zaid, 'Abdullāh bin 'Abbās, Abū Mūsā Al-Ash'arī, Ḥudhaifah bin

61. Tārīkhuṭ-Ṭabarī, vol. 5, pp. 150-151, Dhikru Masīri Mann Sāra Ilā Dhī Khashabin Min Ahli Miṣra....., Published by Dārul-Fikr, Beirut, 2002 edition [Publishers]

Al-Yamān, Abū Hurairah, 'Abdullāh bin Salām, 'Ubādah bin Ṣāmit and Muḥammad bin Maslamah, may Allah be pleased with all of them, not Yazīd bin Qais and Ashtar.

The messenger reached Jazirah with the letter and handed it over to the people who had been exiled from Kufah. When they read it, except for Ashtar, all the others disliked it as they had already witnessed the influence of 'Abdur-Raḥmān bin Khālid. However, as for Ashtar, who had gone to Madinah in order to seek forgiveness from Ḥaḍrat 'Uthmān[ra], was unable to keep his repentance intact and immediately set out for Kufah. When his friends saw that Ashtar had left for Kufah, they became frightened that 'Abdur-Raḥmān would not believe them and think that all of this had taken place on their suggestion. So, out of this fear, these people fled as well. When 'Abdur-Raḥmān bin Khālid bin Walīd learned of this he sent his men in pursuit of them, but they were unable to apprehend them. One *manzil*[62] after another, Mālikul-Ashtar reached Kufah in no time. He deemed it against his honour to enter the city empty handed. This person, who came from Jazirah to meet his companions, having covered two *manzils* at a time as if they were one, began to announce his arrival from Madinah. In order to incite the people, he began to say:

> *"I have just left behind Sa'īd bin Al-'Āṣ[ra], who I accompanied for a distance of one manzil. He openly says, 'I will stain the chastity of the women of Kufah,' and he also says, 'The properties in Kufah are the wealth of the*

62. A distance equivalent to 19 miles or 25 kilometers. [Publishers]

Quraish.' Furthermore, he boastfully recites the following couplet:

وَيْلٌ لِاَشْرَافِ النِّسَاءِ مِنِّىْ   صَمَحْمَحٌ كَأَنَّنِىْ مِنْ جِنّ

Meaning, 'Noble women shall fall to trial because of me! I am a man so powerful as if from among the Jinn.'"[63]

The ordinary masses lost their senses due to his statements and they believed everything that he said. Fury instantly surged forth. The wise and learned tried their utmost to convince them and said, *'This is deception, do not be mislead,'* but who could tame the public outrage; no one paid heed to them. A man stood up and announced:

"Whoever wishes to request the dismissal of Sa'īd bin Al-'Āṣ[ra]*, the governor of Kufah, and the appointment of another governor, should immediately join Yazīd bin Qais."*

People rushed out upon hearing this announcement and no one remained in the mosque except for the learned and noble, and those who were in authority. 'Umar bin Al-Juraid was the acting governor for Sa'īd in his absence. He began to deliver an exhortation to the remaining people and said:

'O people! Remember the favour of God the Exalted upon us when we were enemies. He united your hearts and you became as brothers. You were on the brink of a pit of destruction and God the Exalted saved you from it. So do not cast yourself into the affliction which God the Exalted

63. Tārīkhuṭ-Ṭabarī, vol. 5, pp. 141-142, Dhikrul-Khabari 'An Ijtimā'ihim Li-Dhālika Wa Khabarul-Jur'ati, Published by Dārul-Fikr, Beirut, 2002 edition [Publishers]

has saved you from. Do you not recognise the truth and come to its doorstep after having accepted Islam, receiving divine guidance and in the presence of the sunnah[64] *of the Holy Prophet*[sa]*?'*

Qa'qā' bin 'Amr[ra] responded:

> *"You desire to stop this disorder through admonition, but do not hope of this. Nothing but the sword can stop these disturbances and the time is not far when even the sword will be unsheathed. At that time, these people will cry like lambs and wish that this era should return again but God the Exalted would not bestow this favour upon them again until the Day of Judgment."*

The public gathered outside the town, faced Madinah and began to wait for Sa'īd bin Al-'Āṣ[ra]. When he came before them, they said to him, *"Turn back; we are in no need of you."* Sa'īd replied:

> *"What is the wisdom behind so many people gathering and coming out for this purpose? In order to stop one person, why were a thousand men needed? It would have sufficed you to send a man towards the Khalīfah and a man towards me."*

After saying this he spurred on his mount and returned to Madinah in order to warn Ḥaḍrat 'Uthmān[ra], while these people were left astonished. Shortly thereafter, they spotted one of his servants and killed him.

Sa'īd bin Al-'Āṣ[ra] reached Madinah and informed Ḥaḍrat 'Uthmān[ra] of the entire conflict. Ḥaḍrat 'Uthmān[ra] asked, *"Have they risen up against me?"* Sa'īd replied, *"They make it seem*

64. Practice of the Holy Prophet[sa] [Publishers]

as if a new governor is being requested." He inquired, "*Who do they ask for?*" He replied, "*They prefer Abū Mūsā Al-Ash'ārī.*"

APPOINTMENT OF ABŪ MŪSĀ AL-ASH'ARĪ[RA] AS THE GOVERNOR OF KUFAH

Ḥaḍrat 'Uthmān[ra] said:

"*I appoint Abū Mūsā Al-Ash'arī[ra] as the governor of Kufah. By God, I shall give these people no opportunity to raise an objection or allow them to find fault. In response to their statements I shall demonstrate patience as per the commandment of the Holy Prophet[sa], until the time that they desire arrives, i.e., the removal of 'Uthmān.*"[65]

This conflict disclosed that these people did not even slightly refrain from speaking lies and falsehood.

CONSPIRACIES OF THE REBELS EXPOSED

The fleeing of Mālikul-Ashtar from Jazirah under the pretence of coming from Madinah, levelling a false allegation upon Sa'īd bin Al-'Āṣ[ra], and attributing disgraceful and self-concocted things towards him, were not matters which could allow the true motives and secret intentions of the rebels to remain hidden. In fact, this evidently demonstrates that these people were completely oblivious to Islam. Islam does not permit falsehood, does not advocate deception and slandering is a grave crime in Islam. However, these people, who apparently professed love and indignation for Islam, told lies and slandered

65. Tārīkhuṭ-Ṭabarī, vol. 5, pp. 141-142, Dhikrul-Khabari 'An Ijtimā'ihim Li-Dhālika Wa Khabarul-Jur'ati, Published by Dārul-Fikr, Beirut, 2002 edition [Publishers]

others; and all the while they felt no shame in doing so. Hence, their hue and cry against Ḥaḍrat 'Uthmān[ra] was sufficient proof of the fact that this commotion was not on account of any real shortcoming; rather, it was the result of being distanced from Islam and irreligiousness.

The second conclusion which is derived from this incident is that these people did not possess even a single legitimate complaint against Ḥaḍrat 'Uthmān[ra] and his governors. For if a complaint truly existed, what need was there for them to fabricate lies? The invention of false complaints alone is sufficient evidence of the fact that these people had no real complaint. As such, we see that before the arrival of Ashtar when Yazīd held a gathering, only a few soldiers participated at the time. When Qa'qā' prohibited them, they became afraid and put off their gathering. However, we see that within the very same month after being influenced by the lies of Ashtar a large segment of the public had joined these people and set out from Kufah in order to stop Sa'īd and request the appointment of another governor. This is testimony to the fact that initially, people would not be easily deceived by the rebels because they had no means to incite them. When Ashtar managed to invent a means, which was enough to spark the people's indignation, a section of the public fell into this trap and joined them.

The emergence of this disorder also clearly establishes that the actual opposition of these people was against Ḥaḍrat 'Uthmān[ra] and not his governors. For in the beginning, it was he against whom the rebels desired to incite the people. However, when they noticed that no one would join them in this; rather, they would begin to oppose them, these people began to incite the public against the governors. The fact that the rebels were heading for Madinah with a large party also proves that they did not harbour good intentions for Ḥaḍrat 'Uthmān[ra]. Furthermore, their needlessly killing the freed slave of Sa'īd bin Al-'Āṣ[ra], demonstrates that in order to fulfil their ends these people felt no hindrance in committing any crime whatsoever.

It appears that by now these people had begun to perceive that if there was even a slight delay, the Muslim people would come to learn of the gravity of their mischief. For this reason, they were deeply concerned in attaining their objective in whatever way and as quickly as possible. However, with his wisdom, Ḥaḍrat 'Uthmān[ra] dismissed their excuses once again. He appointed Abū Mūsā Al-Ash'arī[ra] as the governor and immediately informed the people. Their hopes had already been frustrated when Sa'īd bin Al-'Āṣ[ra] returned and informed the people of Madinah of their motives. Their plans under deliberation of suddenly occupying Madinah, were frustrated and they were forced to turn back. Now, with the appointment of Abū Mūsā Al-Ash'arī[ra] as the governor, their objections had been completely done away with because these people desired his appointment as governor for some time.

When Abū Mūsā Al-Ash'arī[ra] came to know of his appointment as the governor of Kufah, he gathered everyone and said:

> *"O people! Never set out for such works again, and adopt unity and obedience. Act patiently and refrain from haste because now an Amir is amongst you i.e. I have been appointed as the Amir."*

Upon this, these people requested him to lead them in prayer but he refused saying, *"No, this will never happen."*[66]

OBEDIENCE TO THE RULER OF THE TIME IS NECESSARY

He went on to state:

> *"I shall not become your Imām until you affirm complete obedience to Ḥaḍrat 'Uthmān*[ra] *and declare that you will accept his orders."*

Upon this, the people promised that they would show complete obedience to him in the future and accept his orders. It was only then that Abū Mūsā Al-Ash'arī[ra] led them in prayer. Similarly, Ḥaḍrat Abū Mūsā[ra] told them:

> *"Hearken! I have heard the Holy Prophet*[sa] *say, 'At a time when people are under an Imām, anyone who rises up to create disaccord among them and to scatter their community, should be executed, whoever he may be.*[67] *The Holy Prophet*[sa] *has not stipulated the condition of the Imām being equitable. In other words, you cannot say that Ḥaḍrat 'Uthmān is not just; for even if this is accepted as being true, your action is still unwarranted because the Holy Prophet*[sa] *has not stipulated the condition of justice.*

66. Tārīkhuṭ-Ṭabarī, vol. 5, p. 142, Dhikrul-Khabari 'An Ijtimā'ihim Li-Dhālika Wa Khabarul-Jur'ati, Published by Dārul-Fikr, Beirut, 2002 edition [Publishers]

67. * Ṣaḥīḥ Muslim, Kitābul-Imārah, Bābu Ḥukmi Man Farraqa Amral-Muslimīna Wa Huwa Mujtami'un, Ḥadīth No. 4796
* Tārīkhuṭ-Ṭabarī, vol. 5, p. 144, Dhikrul-Khabari 'An Ijtimā'ihim Li-Dhālika Wa Khabarul-Jur'ati, Published by Dārul-Fikr, Beirut, 2002 edition [Publishers]

Instead, the Holy Prophet[sa] has merely stated that there should be a ruler over the people."

These were the views of those people who had spent their entire lives in the service of Islam and who had heard the teachings of Islam directly from the lips of the Holy Prophet[sa]. Moreover, they had received an attestation of approval by acting upon these teachings in his presence. What to talk of praying behind these rebels, they did not even desire to become their Imām in prayer and considered them liable for capital punishment. Can it be said about such people that they were a part of the conflict in the era of Ḥaḍrat 'Uthmān[ra] or that Ḥaḍrat 'Uthmān[ra] and his governors were usurping the rights of the citizens? Similarly, in light of these events can it be accepted that these rebels were creating disorder on their behalf. Of course not! In fact, this rebel party was bent upon creating disorder out of its jealousy towards the community of companions and these people hid their heartfelt views. Their real objective was the destruction of the Islamic government and this objective could not be achieved without moving Ḥaḍrat 'Uthmān[ra] aside. Not catching on to their deception, certain ignorant or faithless Muslims, joined them as well either out of their selfishness or simplicity.

ANOTHER CONSPIRACY OF THE MISCHIEF-MAKERS

After the appointment of Ḥaḍrat Abū Mūsā Al-Ash'arī[ra] as governor, there remained no reason for these people to create disorder. However, the real instigators of this conflict could not have been pleased with all their efforts going to waste in this manner. Hence, written correspondence began and it was decided that a few people from all the provinces should set out towards Madinah in the form of delegations. There, they should deliberate as to the future course of action, and certain questions should also be posed to Ḥaḍrat 'Uthmān[ra] so that these discussions may be publicised in all directions and people may become convinced that the allegations levelled against Ḥaḍrat 'Uthmān[ra] have been proven beyond doubt. After deciding the matter they all left their homes and headed for Madinah. When they reached close to Madinah Ḥaḍrat 'Uthmān[ra] learnt of their arrival. He sent two men to enquire about them and ascertain the real purpose of their arrival, and then report back to him. The two of them left and met this caravan outside Madinah. During the course of discussion these people revealed to the two informants their state of affairs. The two of them asked whether anyone from the people of Madinah was with them. This treacherous group replied that there were three people in Madinah and besides them, they did not have a fourth supporter. The two enquired, *"Then what is your intention?"* They replied:

> *"Our intention is to go to Madinah in order to speak to Ḥaḍrat 'Uthmān[ra] regarding certain matters which we have already instilled into the minds of people. Then we will return to our towns and tell everyone that we raised many objections against Ḥaḍrat 'Uthmān[ra] and established their validity, but he has refused to abstain from these things and did not repent. Then we will leave, under the pretence of going for hajj and besiege him upon reaching Madinah. If he steps down from Khilāfat, then well and good, otherwise we will kill him."*

THE CONSPIRACY EXPOSED

Both of these informants returned with a full report of their findings and briefed Ḥaḍrat 'Uthmān[ra]. Upon hearing their state of affairs, Ḥaḍrat 'Uthmān[ra] began to laugh and prayed to God the Exalted, *"O Allah! Save these people from going astray. They will be ruined if You do not save them."* Then, regarding the three men from among the people of Madinah who were with the mischief-makers, he said:

> *"As for 'Ammār, he is angry because he attacked 'Abbās bin 'Utbah bin Abī Lahab and he was reprimanded for this. Whereas Muḥammad bin Abī Bakr has turned arrogant and thinks that no law is binding upon him and Muḥammad bin Abī Ḥudhaifah is putting himself in trouble for no reason."*

Then Ḥaḍrat 'Uthmān[ra] called the mischief-makers and gathered the companions of the Holy Prophet[sa] as well.

ḤAḌRAT 'UTHMĀN[RA] SUMMONS THE MISCHIEF-MAKERS

When everyone had gathered, Ḥaḍrat 'Uthmān[ra] informed them of the whole affair. The two informants also stood by as witnesses and gave their testimony. Upon this, all the companions gave the following verdict:

> *"Execute these people because the Holy Prophet[sa] has said, 'May the curse of Allah be upon such an individual who calls people towards his own obedience or the obedience of another, at a time when there is an Imām who is present. Kill such a person whoever he may be.'"*

Then, they reminded everyone of the words of Ḥaḍrat 'Umar[ra]:

"I do not deem the execution of any such person permissible for you in which I do not have a part."

In other words, no one may be executed unless there is an indication from the government. Upon hearing the verdict of the companions Ḥaḍrat 'Uthmān[ra] stated:

'No, we will forgive them and accept their pleas. We will counsel them with all our efforts and we will not oppose anyone so long as he does not clearly violate the law or express disbelief.'[68]

ḤAḌRAT 'UTHMĀN[RA] CLEARS HIMSELF OF ALL CHARGES

Then Ḥaḍrat 'Uthmān[ra] said:

"These people have mentioned certain things which you are aware of as well. However, their plan is to debate with me on these issues so that they can return and say, 'We engaged in a debate with 'Uthmān regarding these matters and he has been defeated.' These people allege that whilst on journey, I offered the prayer in full but the Holy Prophet[sa] used to perform qaṣr[69] *whilst on journey.*[70] *However, it was only in Minā where I offered the prayer in full and even that was due to two reasons: firstly, because I owned property there and I had married there; secondly,*

68. Tārīkhuṭ-Ṭabarī, vol. 5, p. 151, Dhikru Masīri Mann Sāra Ilā Dhī Khashabin Min Ahli Miṣra....., Published by Dārul-Fikr, Beirut, 2002 edition [Publishers]
69. A shortened version of the obligatory prayer, which is offered as such in certain circumstances. [Publishers]
70. Sunanut-Tirmidhī, Kitābuṣ-Ṣalāh, Abwābus-Safari, Bābu Mā Jā'a Fit-Taqṣīri Fis-Safari, Ḥadīth No. 544

because I came to know that in those days people had converged for the hajj and the uneducated from among them would begin to say that the Khalīfah only offers two rak'āt[71] *so there must only be two rak'āt in the prayer. Is this not true?"*

The companions replied, *"Yes this is correct."* Then Ḥaḍrat 'Uthmān[ra] said:

"The second allegation that they raise is that I have introduced the innovation of establishing public pastures, although this is a false accusation. Pastures were established before me. They were introduced by Ḥaḍrat 'Umar[ra] *and I have only made them more spacious due to the growing number of camels which are given in alms. Then, the land designated for public pastures is not the wealth of anyone. I have no benefit in this; I have only two camels, whereas at the time when I became Khalīfah I was more wealthy then all the Arabs. Now I only have two camels which I have kept for hajj. Is this not true?"*

The noble companions affirmed, *"Indeed, it is."* Then Ḥaḍrat 'Uthmān[ra] said:

"They say that I appoint comparatively young men as governors, even though I only appoint such individuals as governors who posses virtuous attributes and manners. Holy men before me appointed even younger people as governors than those appointed by me. Far more objections were raised against the Holy Prophet[sa] *for appointing*

71. A *rak'at* is a cycle in the formal Muslim—plural *rak'āt* [Publishers]

Usāmah bin Zaid as the General of an army than are now being raised against me. Is this not true?"

The companions responded, *"It is true. These people raise objections before the people but hide the real events."* In this manner Ḥaḍrat 'Uthmān[ra] stated all the objections one by one and refuted them one after another. The companions emphatically persisted that they should be executed, but Ḥaḍrat 'Uthmān[ra] did not agree and released them. Ṭabarī states:

اَبَى الْمُسْلِمُوْنَ اِلَّا قَتْلَهُمْ وَ اَبٰى اِلَّا تَرْكَهُمْ

"The rest of the Muslims were adamant on having them executed but Ḥaḍrat 'Uthmān[ra] could not be convinced in any way to punish them."[72]

ḤAḌRAT 'UTHMĀN[RA] SHOWS MERCY TOWARDS THE MISCHIEF-MAKERS

This incident shows the various types of falsehood and deception which would be employed by the mischief-makers. In that era, when the press and means of transport were not as developed as today, it was very easy for these people to mislead the uneducated. In reality, however, these people had no legitimate reason to rise up. Neither did the truth support them nor did they speak the truth. All their endeavours were founded upon lies and falsehood. It was only the mercy of Ḥaḍrat 'Uthmān[ra] that was saving them, otherwise, the Muslims would have torn them to pieces. The companions could not have ever

72. Tārīkhuṭ-Ṭabarī, vol. 5, pp. 151-152, Dhikru Masīri Mann Sāra Ilā Dhī Khashabin Min Ahli Miṣra....., Published by Dārul-Fikr, Beirut, 2002 edition [Publishers]

tolerated that the peace and security which they had achieved by sacrificing their lives be done away with in this manner by the mischief of a few wicked people. They could see that the Islamic state would crumble if these people were not promptly punished. However, Ḥaḍrat 'Uthmān[ra] was an embodiment of mercy and he desired, in any way possible, for these people to be rightly guided so that they would not die in a state of disbelief. As such, Ḥaḍrat 'Uthmān[ra] would show leniency towards these people and looked upon their actions of manifest rebellion as a mere intention to commit rebellion, and would put off their punishment.

This incident also illustrates that the companions greatly detested these people. The reason being that firstly, the mischief-makers stated themselves that only three people of Madinah were with them and no more. If other companions were also on their side, they would have named them as well. Secondly, the companions demonstrated through their actions as well that they abhorred the actions of these mischief-makers; and looked upon their deeds as being in violation of the shariah to such extent, that in their view, no punishment lesser than execution was acceptable. If the companions supported these people or the people of Madinah held the same views as the mischief-makers, they would not have needed any further justification or excuse; and would have killed Ḥaḍrat 'Uthmān[ra] there and then, and elected another person for the office of *Khilāfat* in his stead. However, we observe that instead of these people being successful in killing Ḥaḍrat 'Uthmān, may Allah be pleased with him, their very own lives became endangered by the unsheathed swords of the companions. It was only due to the favour and kindness of the very same gracious and compassionate person—whom they sought to murder and against whom they had instigated an outrage—that they were able to safely escape. One is astonished at the malice and unrighteousness of these mischief-makers, for they did not derive the slightest benefit from this incident. Each and every one of their allegations was amply refuted and all their objections were proven to be false and unfounded. They witnessed the mercy and compassion of Ḥaḍrat 'Uthmān[ra] and the soul of every individual bore witness to the fact that the likes of such a person cannot be found on the face of the earth at this time. However, instead of repenting for their sins, being ashamed of their cruelties, feeling remorse for their trespasses and refraining from their mischief, these people began to burn even more in the fire of rage and fury. They considered their being rendered speechless a disgrace and the forgiveness of Ḥaḍrat 'Uthmān[ra] as being the result of their good planning. As such, they returned whilst devising strategies to fulfil their remaining plan in the future.[73]

ANOTHER GRAVE CONSPIRACY BY THE MISCHIEF-MAKERS

After returning, these people began to engage in written correspondence again. Ultimately, it was decided that according to their initial plan, in *Shawwāl*, everyone would set out in the form of a caravan under the pretence of performing hajj and then enter Madinah where they would suddenly upset

73. Tārīkhuṭ-Ṭabarī, vol. 5, p. 152, Dhikru Masīri Mann Sāra Ilā Dhī Khashabin Min Ahli Miṣra....., Published by Dārul-Fikr, Beirut, 2002 edition [Publishers]

the entire system and change the system of government as per their own liking. According to this proposal, in *Shawwāl*, i.e. the tenth lunar month, in the twelfth year of the *Khilāfat* of Ḥaḍrat 'Uthmān[ra] or 36 A.H., the rebels left their homes in the form of three caravans. One caravan was from Basrah, one from Kufah and one from Egypt. Keeping in mind the previous failure and considering that this was a final attempt, 'Abdullāh bin Sabā also left for Madinah along with the caravan from Egypt. The chief of the rebels stepping out himself, was an indication of the fact that these people would now attempt to achieve their objective with the use of every possible tactic. As all the parties had outwardly expressed their intention of going for hajj in their respective regions, other people who actually intended to perform hajj also joined them. In this manner, their true intentions remained hidden from the ordinary Muslims. However, since the governors knew of their internal conspiracy, 'Abdullāh bin Abī Sarah, the governor of Egypt, dispatched a special emissary to inform Ḥaḍrat 'Uthmān[ra] of the caravan and their intentions in good time and the people of Madinah became vigilant.

At this instance, the question arises that when the people of Madinah and especially the companions desired to execute these mischief-makers upon their arrival to Madinah on three separate occasions; and whereas the rebels knew that Ḥaḍrat 'Uthmān[ra] was well aware of their plan of coming and creating disorder under the pretence of performing hajj, why then did these people set out according to their initial plan, which Ḥaḍrat 'Uthmān[ra] was well aware of, instead of devising another plan? Does this mean that in actuality the people of Madinah were with these mischief-makers and this is why they were not afraid?

The answer to this question is that no doubt, this audacity of theirs demonstrates that they had full confidence in their victory. However, the reason for this was not because the companions or the people of Madinah were with them or expressed sympathy for them; rather, as is evident from their own statement, only three people of Madinah were with them. Furthermore, as events establish, the companions as well as the other residents of Madinah were extremely averse to these people. Hence, the reason for their daring behaviour cannot be due to the fact that the companions or the people of Madinah expressed any kind of sympathy towards them. The actual reason for the boldness of these people was firstly the mercy of Ḥaḍrat ‘Uthmān[ra]. The mischief-makers thought that if they were successful then the objective had been achieved, but if they failed, they would escape punishment by appealing to the mercy of Ḥaḍrat ‘Uthmān[ra].

Secondly, although the rebels had witnessed the reaction of the companions and people of Madinah on the previous occasion and they knew that Ḥaḍrat ‘Uthmān[ra] was aware of their arrival, these people thought that he would not mobilise an army to fight them due to his forbearance and the companions would not confront them. Considering the companions to be like themselves, the mischief-makers assumed that the companions only apparently expressed loyalty towards Ḥaḍrat ‘Uthmān[ra] but actually desired his destruction. This assumption was based on the fact that the mischief-makers would give the impression that they were doing everything in order to safeguard the rights of the companions. Hence, they thought that the companions were moved by the influence of their deceit and felt sympathy for them at heart.

ARRIVAL OF THE MISCHIEF-MAKERS IN MADINAH

As soon as word came that this army had reached close to Madinah, the companions and the people of Madinah, who had gone out to manage their properties and lands in the surrounding area, congregated in Madinah. Their army was divided into two groups: one set out from Madinah to fight the rebels while the second force remained in the city for the protection of Ḥaḍrat 'Uthmān[ra]. When all three caravans arrived close to Madinah, the rebels of Basrah settled at a place known as Dhū-Khashab, the rebels of Kufah at A'was and the rebels of Egypt at Dhul-Marwah. They consulted one another as to what they should do next. Even though their number is estimated to have been from between eighteen hundred to three thousand men (the other pilgrims who set out along with them, considering them to be a hajj caravan, were separate), the rebels thought that fighting the valiant men of Islam would not be easy if they were determined to fight. For this reason, they deemed it essential to immediately gather the view of the people of Madinah upon entering the city. As such, two men named Ziyād bin An-Naḍr and 'Abdullāh bin Al-Aṣam advised the rebels of Kufah and Basrah that it was not wise to be hasty and if they rushed things, then the rebels of Egypt would also have to hurry and the plan would be ruined. They replied:

"We have learnt that the people of Madinah have prepared an army against us. If they have prepared to such a great extent despite not being fully aware of our circumstances, they will become even more vigilant upon learning of our complete state of affairs. Our victory shall become a

mere dream. Therefore, it is more appropriate for us to first go there and ascertain the circumstances and speak to the people of Madinah. If they consider it unacceptable to fight us and the reports that we have received about them prove false, we will return and inform you of all the circumstances and appropriate action will be taken."

Everyone was in favour of this proposal. So the two of them went to Madinah and first met the *azwāj-e-muṭahharāt*[74] of the Holy Prophet[sa]. They asked them for permission to enter Madinah and claimed that they had only come in order to request Ḥaḍrat 'Uthmān[ra] to change certain governors and that they held no other intentions. All the wives of the Holy Prophet[sa] refused to accept their words and said that the consequences of such action would not be favourable. Then they approached Ḥaḍrat 'Alī[ra], Ḥaḍrat Ṭalḥah[ra] and Ḥaḍrat Zubair[ra] one by one and sought permission to enter Madinah stating the same reason for their arrival and apparently exhibiting good intention. However, these three companions also refused to fall into their deceit and plainly responded that there was no good in this design of theirs.[75]

After ascertaining the state of affairs in Madinah and having failed in their objective, when both these men returned and informed their comrades of the complete situation, a few leading men from all three regions of Kufah, Basrah and Egypt arrived in Madinah to make the final attempt. In accordance

74. The noble wives of the Holy Prophet [Publishers]
75. Tārīkhuṭ-Ṭabarī, vol. 5, pp. 152-153, Dhikru Masīri Mann Sāra Ilā Dhī Khashabin Min Ahli Miṣra....., Published by Dārul-Fikr, Beirut, 2002 edition

with the teachings of 'Abdullāh bin Sabā the rebels of Egypt believed Ḥaḍrat 'Alī[ra] to be the *waṣī* of the Holy Prophet[sa] and were not ready to perform *bai'at*[76] on the hand of anyone other than him. However, although the rebels of Kufah and Basrah were with them as far as the uprising was concerned, they were not at agreement as far as belief was concerned. Thus, the people of Kufah considered it to be in their best interest to offer *bai'at* to Zubair bin 'Awwām[ra] and the people of Basrah looked upon Ṭalḥah[ra]. Due to this disagreement the representatives of each caravan turned to those individuals whom they wished to appoint for the office of *Khilāfat* after Ḥaḍrat 'Uthmān[ra].

THE REBELS OF EGYPT APPROACH ḤAḌRAT 'ALĪ[RA]

The rebels of Egypt went to Ḥaḍrat 'Alī[ra], who was commanding a section of the army outside Madinah at the time, which stood ready to crush the rebels. They approached him and said that Ḥaḍrat 'Uthmān[ra] was no longer suitable for *Khilāfat* due to his administrative incompetence and that they had come to dismiss him and hoped that Ḥaḍrat 'Alī[ra] would accept this office after him. Upon hearing their proposal, he demonstrated such a degree of religious indignation as befitted a man of his stature. Thus, he rebuked them and acted very harshly towards them saying:

> *"All pious people know that the Holy Prophet[sa] has foretold of the armies that would setup camp in Dhul-Marwah and Dhū Khashab (where the rebels had setup camp) and*

76. An oath of allegience to a religious leader. [Publishers]

> *then invoked curse upon them.*[77] *Hence, may God ruin you! Be Gone!"*

They replied, *"Very well, we shall return."* After this, they returned.

THE REBELS OF KUFAH APPROACH ḤAḌRAT ZUBAIR[RA]

The rebels of Kufah approached Ḥaḍrat Zubair[ra] and submitted, *"Accept the office of Khilāfat after it has been vacated."* He also treated them in the same manner as Ḥaḍrat 'Ali[ra]. He treated them very harshly and rebuked them saying:

> *"All the believers know that the Holy Prophet*[sa] *has said that the armies to setup camp at Dhul-Marwah, Dhū Khashab and A'was would be accursed."*

THE REBELS OF BASRAH APPROACH ḤAḌRAT ṬALḤAH[RA]

Similarly, the rebels of Basrah approached Ḥaḍrat Ṭalḥah, may Allah be pleased with him and he also cast them off. He then informed them of the prophecy of the Holy Prophet[sa] and of his invoking curse upon them.[78]

---

77. Al-Bidāyatu Wan-Nihāyah, By Ḥāfiẓ Ibni Kathīr Dimashqi, vol. 7, p. 169, Sanatu 35 Hijrī, Dhikru Majī'il-Aḥzābi Ilā 'Uthmānu Lil-Marratith-Thāniyati Mim-Miṣra (Wa Ghairihā Fī Shawwālī Min Hādhihis-Sanah), Darul-Kutubil-'Ilmiyyah, Beirut, 2001 edition,
78. Tārīkhuṭ-Ṭabarī, vol. 5, pp. 152-153, Dhikru Masīri Mann Sāra Ilā Dhī Khashabin Min Ahli Miṣra....., Published by Dārul-Fikr, Beirut, 2002 edition

APPOINTMENT OF MUḤAMMAD BIN ABĪ BAKR AS THE GOVERNOR OF EGYPT

When the rebels witnessed this state of affairs and were completely disappointed in this regard, they employed the strategy of expressing remorse for their action and only requested that a few governors be changed. When Ḥaḍrat 'Uthmān, may Allah be pleased with him, learnt of this he accepted their request with extreme affection and kindness. According to the request of these people, Ḥaḍrat 'Uthmān[ra] changed 'Abdullāh bin Abī Saraḥ, the governor of Egypt and appointed Muḥammad bin Abī Bakr in his stead. Upon this, they returned seemingly content and the people of Madinah were joyful that God had saved Islam from a grave conflict. Whatever they had perceived, however, was not correct because these rebels harboured other intentions and none of their activities were free from sedition and disorder.

REALITY BEHIND CONFLICTING NARRATIONS

One should remember that this is the juncture where extreme contradictions in narrations begins. The events which I have just mentioned have been described by various narrators in different ways to such extent that the truth has been veiled completely and many people have been mislead. They have either come to believe that the companions were involved in the entire affair or that in the least, they held a heartfelt sympathy for the rebels. However, this is not correct. A great deal of caution is required with respect to the history of this era, because no era has followed after the one under discussion, which has been absent of such people who held sympathy for either one party or the other. This fact proves to be very detrimental to history because when intense hatred or undue love is involved, a narration can never be transmitted in its true form. Even if a narrator does not speak falsehood, his narration is sure to carry a tinge of his thoughts. Moreover, the particulars of the narrators of history are not as clear as those of hadith. Although historians have taken a great deal of care, they are still unable to establish the authenticity of a narration in the likeness of broad day light, as can be done in the case of hadith. So, a great deal of caution is necessary.

A GOLDEN PRINCIPLE FOR THE VERIFICATION OF HISTORY

However, it is not impossible to ascertain the true facts either because God the Exalted has left open such means by which the true course of events may be very well discerned. Such narrators also exist, who due to being completely neutral, state the facts as they are. A golden principal for the verification of history is that world events are like a chain. In order to verify the authenticity of an individual incident, it should be examined after being threaded into this chain to see whether the link can be threaded into its proper place or not. In order to distinguish between true and false events, this is a very useful aid.

Therefore, caution is required in order to learn about the true course of events pertaining to this era, and there is a need for scrutiny and cross-examination. Without keeping in mind the sequence of events, one cannot learn about the history of any era, especially the one under discussion. Furthermore, taking advantage of this contradiction [in narrations], European writers have distorted the history of that era to such extent that the heart of a Muslim, who possesses indignation, burns when reading these incidents. Additionally, many people who are weak in faith become averse to Islam. It is a pity that even some Muslim historians have carelessly stumbled in this regard and have become the cause of misguiding others.

EXONERATION OF ḤAḌRAT 'UTHMĀN[RA] & THE OTHER COMPANIONS

In this short time I cannot entirely discuss the errors which these people are entangled in. However, I shall briefly present a true account of the circumstances before you, which prove that Ḥaḍrat 'Uthmān[ra] and the other companions were free from every form of mischief and sin. In fact, their behaviour was a manifestation of very high morals and they stood upon a lofty pedestal of virtue.

THE REBELS ENTER MADINAH AGAIN

I have already mentioned that the rebels returned to their homes while apparently displaying agreement; the rebels of Kufah returned Kufah, the rebels of Basrah towards Basrah and the rebels of Egypt towards Egypt. Upon witnessing this state of peace and security, and feeling relieved upon the withdrawal of the rebels, the people of Madinah returned to their tasks. However, many days had not passed - at a time when the people of Madinah were either engaged in their work, or sitting in their homes and mosques, and had no idea whatsoever that the enemy would invade Madinah — that the rebel army suddenly entered

Madinah and besieged the mosque as well as the home of Ḥaḍrat 'Uthmān[ra]. It was announced in all the streets of Madinah that whosoever cherished his life should quietly sit at home and not confront the rebels, or else.[79] Their arrival was so sudden that the people of Madinah were unable to fight back. Ḥaḍrat Imam Ḥasan[ra] states:

> *"I was sitting in the mosque, when all of a sudden there was a clamour and cries of takbīr*[80] *(this was the Muslim slogan for war) began to resonate in the streets of Madinah. All of us were shocked and we began to look for the cause of this noise. I stood up on my knees and began to look. In no time, these people suddenly raided the mosque and occupied it along with the surrounding streets."*

As a result of their sudden attack the force of the companions and the people of Madinah, was scattered. They were unable to fight the rebels or engage in battle with them, because the rebels had besieged the mosque and all the passages of the city. Now there were only two possibilities: firstly, that aid arrived from the exterior; secondly, that the people of Madinah gathered somewhere and then fought them in an organised manner.

As for the first case, the rebels were satisfied that Ḥaḍrat 'Uthmān[ra] would not do such a thing because he was very generous in his mercy and thinking well of others and because he always gave the benefit of the doubt to them despite their apparent mischief. As regards the second case, the rebels made an

---

79. Tārīkhuṭ-Ṭabarī, vol. 5, pp. 153-154, Dhikru Masīri Mann Sāra Ilā Dhī Khashabin Min Ahli Miṣra....., Published by Dārul-Fikr, Beirut, 2002 edition [Publishers]

80. To proclaim the greatness of Allah. [Publishers]

arrangement whereby they kept a stern watch over the streets of Madinah and its entrances, and ordered that no groups should be allowed to assemble anywhere. The rebels would scatter people wherever they happened to gather. However, they would not prohibit the odd conversation here and there, or the meeting of one or two people among themselves.

THE PEOPLE OF MADINAH ADVISE THE REBELS

When the astonishment of the people of Madinah had abated to some extent, a few of them came to the mosque – where the centre of the rebels was – and began to advise them and expressed displeasure towards their action. However, instead of deriving benefit from their admonition, the rebels intimidated and threatened them, and bluntly said that if they did not remain silent, then the consequences would not be good, and they would be harshly dealt with.

THE REBELS TAKE CONTROL OF MADINAH

Now, it was as if Madinah no longer remained to be the headquarters of *Khilāfat*. The rule of the *Khalīfah* of the time had been abolished and a small party of rebels did as they pleased. Be it the companions of the Holy Prophet[sa] or the people of Madinah – all struggled to defend their honour. Upon witnessing this conflict, some even stopped coming out of their homes. They would sit at home, aghast, night and day.[81]

81. Tārīkhuṭ-Ṭabarī, vol. 5, pp. 154-155, Dhikru Masīri Mann Sāra Ilā Dhī Khashabin Min Ahli Miṣra....., Published by Dārul-Fikr, Beirut, 2002 edition

THE MOST PROMINENT COMPANIONS ASK THE REBELS THE REASON FOR THEIR RETURN

On the previous occasion, since the rebels returned expressing their satisfaction and they had no remaining complaints, the companions were surprised as to the real cause of their return. Most did not have the courage to speak before the rebels. A few prominent companions, in whose names the rebels sought refuge and whom they professed to love, enquired of them, *"After all, what is the reason for your return?"* Hence, Ḥaḍrat 'Alī[ra], Ḥaḍrat Ṭalḥah[ra] and Ḥaḍrat Zubair[ra] were the ones to enquire from these people as to reason for their return. They all unanimously replied:

> *"We were returning to our homes with complete satisfaction and assurance when we noticed a person who was mounted on a camel given as ṣadaqah.*[82] *At times he would come in front of us and at times he would fall back. When some of our men noticed him, they became suspicious and apprehended him. When he was questioned as to whether he had a letter, he declined. Furthermore, when it was inquired of him as to the purpose of his journey, he said that he was unaware. This made them even more suspicious. Finally, when he was searched, a letter was found to be in his possession, which was written by Ḥaḍrat 'Uthmān*[ra]*. In it the governor of Egypt had been instructed, 'When the rebels return to Madinah kill so and so, lash so and so and shave their heads and beards, and consider the letter which they are carrying with respect to your dismissal as*

82. Almsgiving in Islam [Publishers]

being invalid.' When we saw this letter we were extremely surprised and returned at once."

Upon hearing this story, Ḥaḍrat 'Alī[ra] instantly retorted:

"This tale has been fabricated in Madinah. O people of Kufah and O people of Basrah! How did you learn that the people of Egypt had seized such a letter despite being at a distance of many manzils from each other? Moreover, how then was it possible for you to return so soon?"

Neither could they respond to this objection, nor was there an answer. So the only reply they could give was, *"Say whatever you like and think of us as you wish. We dislike the Khilāfat of this person. He should resign from his post."*[83] Ka'b bin Ashraf, who held the position of a king among the Jews, was a bitter enemy of the Holy Prophet[sa] and Islam. When his mischief crossed all bounds and the suffering of the Muslims knew no limits Muḥammad bin Maslamah[ra], who was from among the prominent companions and the community of the *anṣār*, had done a great service to Islam by killing him under the instruction of the Holy Prophet[sa]. He made the same argument when he heard of this incident raised the same objection and plainly said, *"This is nothing more than a self-concocted lie."*

ḤAḌRAT 'UTHMĀN[RA] CLEARS HIMSELF OF THE ALLEGATIONS LEVELLED BY THE REBELS

Even though the companions had logically dismissed their tale, the audacity of the rebels had now crossed all limits.

83. Tārīkhuṭ-Ṭabarī, vol. 5, p. 154, Dhikru Masīri Mann Sāra Ilā Dhī Khashabin Min Ahli Miṣra....., Published by Dārul-Fikr, Beirut, 2002 edition [Publishers]

Despite the humiliation they had faced, the rebels presented this matter before Ḥaḍrat 'Uthmān[ra] and demanded an answer from him. At the time, many prominent companions were also present in his company. Ḥaḍrat 'Uthmān[ra] responded:

> *"According to the Islamic shariah there are only two ways to decide a matter. Either the claimant must present two witnesses or an oath must be taken by the defendant. It is obligatory upon you, therefore, to present two witnesses in support of your claim. If not, I swear by that God, beside Whom there is none worthy of worship, that neither have I written this letter, nor has it been written with my consent, nor have I instructed someone to write it, nor am I aware as to who has written this letter."*

He further added, *"You are aware that at times, letters can be forged and stamps may be replicated."* When the companions heard this reply by Ḥaḍrat 'Uthmān[ra], they testified to his truth and declared him innocent of the charges. However, this had no effect on the rebels and why would it; for it was they, who had themselves forged the letter. One can wake a person who is asleep, but how can such a person be awakened who pretends to be asleep, while he is actually awake. The leaders of the rebels understood very well that this was their own deceit. How could they contemplate the validity and logic of these answers? Their followers had become their slaves, they would listen and obey, and accept whatever they were told.

REALITY BEHIND THE REBEL SCHEME

It was neither possible for the rebels to be affected, nor were they effected. However, as for those gifted with insight, this response of Ḥaḍrat 'Uthmān[ra] was so replete of the exemplary attributes of humility and modesty that the audacity and shamelessness of these rebels becomes even more evident. The rebels forged a letter and accused Ḥaḍrat 'Uthmān, may Allah be pleased with him, of deception and lies. Furthermore, Ḥaḍrat 'Alī[ra] and Muḥammad bin Maslamah[ra] deduced [the true state of affairs] from the events and openly charged the rebels of deceit. Even Ḥaḍrat 'Uthmān[ra] himself, who was being accused and against whom this conspiracy was being hatched, cleared himself of the charges, but never said, 'You have forged this letter.' In fact, he actually covered their mistake by merely stating, *"You are aware that a letter can resemble another, a stamp can be replicated, and even a camel can be stolen."*

Some people, who believe Ḥaḍrat 'Uthmān[ra] to be absolved of this allegation but are also inclined to think positively about the rebels, believe that perhaps Marwān wrote this letter and sent it on his own accord. However, in my view this notion is absolutely false. The events clearly show that this letter was forged by the rebels themselves, and was not written by Marwān or any other person. Furthermore, it is also wrong to object that if the rebels had forged this letter, how then did the servant of Ḥaḍrat 'Uthmān[ra] and a camel given in *ṣadaqah* come into their custody; how did they forge the letter of a scribe of Ḥaḍrat 'Uthmān[ra]; and how was it stamped by the ring of Ḥaḍrat 'Uthmān? For many reasons exist, which suggest that it was the rebels who had forged this letter. It appears, however, from the events and seems most likely that this deception was the work of a few leaders alone. It would not be surprising if this was the doing of 'Abdullāh bin Sabā alone and a few of his intimate accomplices; and that the other rebels, even if they were army chiefs, had no knowledge of this.

SEVEN ARGUMENTS IN SUPPORT OF THE 'LETTER CONSPIRACY'

Evidence of the fact that this scheme was the work of the rebels themselves is as follows:

It has already been proven with relation to the rebels that they did not refrain from lying in order to achieve their ends just as they had lied in opposition to Walīd bin 'Utbah and Sa'īd bin Al-'Āṣ. Similarly, they publicised false complaints regarding various foreign administrations, which were investigated by the prominent companions and found to be false. Thus, when it has been established with relation to the rebels that they did not refrain from lying, there is no reason why they should not be held liable in this case either and such people against whom no charge has ever been established should be held responsible.

Just as Ḥaḍrat 'Alī[ra] and Muḥammad bin Maslamah[ra] objected, the prompt return of these rebels and their entrance into Madinah together is a testimony to the fact that this was a conspiracy. The reason being that as history establishes, the rebels of Egypt asserted that they intercepted a messenger at a place known as Buwaib who, according to their statement, was taking the letter of Ḥaḍrat 'Uthmān[ra] to the governor of Egypt.[84] Buwaib is situated at a distance of at least six *manzils* from Madinah – where the route to Egypt begins.[85] If the people of Egypt had reached this far, both the people of Kufah and Basrah must have covered about six *manzils* each in opposite directions as well. Therefore, news of what transpired before the rebels of Egypt could have reached the other two caravans no earlier than within twelve or thirteen days; and taking into account the time spent in leaving [Madinah] and returning, the rebels could not have returned to Madinah in less than twenty-four days, more or less. However, the rebels returned to Madinah in a much shorter time period than this. Hence, it is clearly evident that even before leaving Madinah, the rebels had planned amongst themselves that all the caravans would return on a particular date and suddenly take over Madinah. 'Abdullāh bin Sabā was with the Egyptian caravan and since he was very cunning, he knew that on the one hand people would question them as to why they had returned unnecessarily, and on the other hand he was concerned that the question of why the treaty had been broken after a decision had been made, would weigh heavily upon the conscience of his own men. Hence, he produced a forged letter and mislead the sensibilities of his own men, further igniting the fire of rage and fury in their hearts. After all, it is not difficult to

84. Tārīkhuṭ-Ṭabarī, vol. 5, p. 170, Dhikrul-Khabari 'An Qatlihī Wa Kaifa Qutila, Published by Dārul-Fikr, Beirut, 2002 edition [Publishers]

85. Mu'jamul-Buldān, vol. 1, part 2, p. 403, under the word 'Al-Buwaib,' Published by Dāru Iḥyā'it-Turāthil-Arabiyy, Beirut [Publishers]

steal a camel given in *ṣadaqah* and bring a slave on board through bribery.

The manner in which the incident of the interception of this letter is narrated, is itself unnatural. For if Ḥaḍrat 'Uthmān[ra] or Marwān had sent such a letter why then would the servant come in front of the rebels at times and hide at other times. This behaviour can only be of such a person who wishes to get himself caught. According to the rebels, this servant had been ordered to reach Egypt before the arrival of their caravan. How then can the notion be entertained that he travelled side by side along with the caravan after reaching the location of Buwaib, which is the gate to Egypt. There is a great difference between the journey of a man and a caravan; a caravan cannot travel at the same speed as one man. The reason being that a caravan has many requirements and all the mounts in a caravan are not equally as swift. So, how could it be possible for the messenger to still be with the caravan when it reached Buwaib? At that time, he should have been close to his final destination. The state of the messenger, as described by them, can be attributed to a spy but not a messenger. Similarly, when the messenger was apprehended, the dialogue that took place with him is completely unnatural. This is because he claims to be a messenger, but neither has he been given a letter nor a verbal message. Who can give such a reply except such a person who is either insane or wishes to make himself seem suspicious? If the person really was a messenger what need was there for him to say that he had been sent by Ḥaḍrat 'Uthmān[ra] or someone else. Likewise, it cannot be said that he was well committed to speaking the truth either because it is said that he possessed a letter but the messenger claimed that he was not in the possession of a letter. So according to their narration it is evident that the messenger did in fact speak a lie. The question that subsequently arises is why he would fabricate something which in turn would clearly lead to his capture? Why did he not speak a lie which would save him from being detained in such a situation? Hence, all these occurrences show that the entire affair about the letter and the person carrying it, was a fabrication from beginning to end. Therefore, someone from among the rebels themselves (most probably 'Abdullāh bin Sabā) forged a letter and handed it to a messenger so that he should travel closely in line with the caravan. However, it was not probable for a rider passing by on a heavily used route to be noticed and apprehended. However, since the person who forged this letter desired, insofar as possible, that this should happen through the agency of someone else, he instructed the emissary to move along with the caravan in such a manner that suspicion would arise in the hearts of people; and when they would question him in order to remove their doubt, the emissary should give such answers which would further increase this suspicion. The general public would search the emissary themselves and upon finding the letter would be certain that Ḥaḍrat 'Uthmān[ra] had deceived them.

The contents of the letter also indicate that it was a counterfeit and was not crafted by a well-versed Muslim, because in certain narrations the subject matter of the letter reads that the beard of so and so should be shaved. However, the shaving of one's beard is prohibited in Islam and under the Islamic rule, only such punishments could be meted out which were in accordance with Islam. It was absolutely unacceptable for a person to be made to eat swine, drink alcohol or to shave his beard as a form of punishment, because all these things were forbidden [in Islam]. The only punishments evident in Islam are those of execution, corporal punishment, fine or expulsion from the land, whether it be in the form of exile or imprisonment. No other punishment is proven to have been administered in Islam except for the ones just mentioned. Neither did the Islamic scholars ever impose such a punishment, nor Ḥaḍrat 'Uthmān[ra] himself, nor his governors. As such, for such a punishment to be written in this letter is sufficient proof of the fact that the letter was forged by someone who was unacquainted with the essence of Islam.

The events preceding this letter also refute the possibility of it being from Ḥaḍrat 'Uthmān[ra] or his secretary, because all narrations unanimously agree that Ḥaḍrat 'Uthmān[ra] exhibited a great deal of leniency in punishing the rebels. If he had wished, Ḥaḍrat 'Uthmān[ra] could have executed them all at the first instance of their arrival. Then, if Ḥaḍrat 'Uthmān[ra] had left them on that occasion, the ringleaders could have most surely been arrested on their arrival a second time, because then they had openly committed an act of rebellion; and the companions were ready to fight them. However, to believe that he showed the rebels leniency at this stage but wrote a letter to the governor of Egypt that he should punish them, is a remarkably irrational notion. Similarly, it cannot be asserted that Marwān wrote this letter in view of the leniency of Ḥaḍrat 'Uthmān[ra], because Marwān knew well that Ḥaḍrat 'Uthmān[ra] was very strict in guarding the penal code. The conscience of Marwān could not have allowed him to think for even a minute that he would remain safe from punishment after writing such a letter. Then, if he were to write such a letter, why would he only write one to the governor of Egypt? Why did he not write similar letters to the governors of Basrah and Kufah as well? In this way all the enemies would have been dealt with once and for all. The fact that a letter was only written to the governor of Egypt is evidence of the fact that the caravans of Kufah and Basrah did not have in their midst a man as cunning as Abdullāh bin Sabā.

One may assert that perhaps similar instructions were issued to the governors of both these regions as well, but the people who were carrying them could not been apprehended. The answer is that if this were the case then the matter could not have remained hidden. If 'Abdullāh bin 'Āmir is accused of remaining silent due to being a relative of Ḥaḍrat 'Uthmān[ra], then Ḥaḍrat Abū Mūsā Al-Ash'arī[ra], who was from among the prominent companions; whose impeccable faith has been testified to in the Holy Quran and who was the governor of Kufah at the time, would never have remained silent, and would have surely disclosed the matter. Hence, the truth is that this letter was forged and had been crafted by someone from within the Egyptian caravan. Aside from the Egyptian caravan, since there was neither such a person present in the other caravans as was capable of carrying out such a scheme, nor was it possible to steal so many camels from *baitul-māl* in such a short time, nor could so many slaves be bribed; for this reason, letters addressed to the governors of other regions were not forged.

The servant about whom it was suggested that he carried this letter, could have shed the most light on this matter. However, it is surprising that when Ḥaḍrat 'Uthmān[ra] demanded for witnesses this servant was neither presented, nor is there any mention of him in the events that followed. This indicates that it was not in their best interest to present him. Perhaps they feared that he would disclose the true state of affairs before the companions. Therefore, keeping him hidden is a testimony to the fact that it was the rebel party themselves, who was responsible for forging this letter.

A very compelling proof of the fact that these people had forged this letter themselves is that this was not the first letter which they had crafted. In fact, they had forged many other letters in addition to this, in order to ignite the flames of the very same disorder. Hence, it was neither difficult for them to craft this letter, nor can this be attributed to anyone else in the presence of this reality. The counterfeit letters which these people had been producing previously were written [falsely on behalf of] Ḥaḍrat 'Alī[ra] in order to defame him, and the contents of these letters was along the lines of, *'Incite rage against Ḥaḍrat 'Uthmān[ra].'* The vehemence of the general public was instigated through these letters and upon seeing the attestation of Ḥaḍrat 'Alī[ra] [on these letters] they would fall for the words of 'Abdullāh bin Sabā. However, it appears that they were ordered to keep the content of the letters very secret, lest Ḥaḍrat 'Alī[ra] found out about them and rejected having any connection with them. Furthermore, the masterminds behind this disorder presented a valid reason for their emphasis upon secrecy, i.e. [they claimed that] if these letters were exposed then Ḥaḍrat 'Alī[ra] would be confronted with difficulty. For this reason, people would not disclose the subject matter of these letters for the sake of Ḥaḍrat 'Alī[ra] and since the matter was kept secret, the deception of the masterminds would not be disclosed either. However, falsehood never remains hidden for long, especially when hundreds are made aware of it. The letter which was supposedly written on behalf of Ḥaḍrat 'Uthmān[ra] was seized and the ordinary masses of Kufah turned back extremely enraged. A group of them approached Ḥaḍrat 'Alī[ra] and asked for his assistance. Ḥaḍrat 'Alī[ra] had become aware of the falsity of this account as soon as he heard about it, and due to his God-given insight, the deception of the rebels of Egypt had become evident to him. He plainly refused saying, *"I cannot join you in such a thing."* At the time, in the heat of their emotion, some were unable to exercise caution and spontaneously said, *"Then why have you been sending us letters?"* This was very surprising for Ḥaḍrat 'Alī[ra]. He plainly rejected this, expressed his ignorance and said, *"I swear by God the Exalted! I have never written any such letter to you people."* These people were also extremely shocked because in actuality, they had also been deceived themselves. They began to look at one another in amazement and enquired, *"Is this the person for whom you express rage and fight?"* In other words, this was to say that, God-forbid, Ḥaḍrat 'Alī[ra] was such a coward that after having done everything, he was now wiping his hands clean.[86]

It appears from this incident that there were certain people from among the rebels who were skilled in crafting counterfeit letters and that such people were present among the people of Egypt. The reason being that these letters could only be written on behalf of Ḥaḍrat 'Alī[ra] to the Egyptians, who

---

86. Tārīkhuṭ-Ṭabarī, vol. 5, pp. 156-157, Dhikru Masīri Mann Sāra Ilā Dhī Khashabin Min Ahli Miṣra....., Published by Dārul-Fikr, Beirut, 2002 edition [Publishers]

professed their love for Ḥaḍrat 'Alī[ra]. Hence, the fact that the letter attributed to Ḥaḍrat 'Uthmān[ra] was seized by the Egyptian caravan is overwhelming evidence that the person who wrote it was not a person from Madinah; rather, he belonged to the caravan from Egypt.

Since the 'letter incident' is the most significant occurrence in the eyes of those who raise an allegation against Ḥaḍrat 'Uthmān, may Allah be pleased with him, I have expounded my research on this incident in detail. Although this incident can be described even more extensively, I believe that what I have mentioned thus far is sufficient to prove that this letter was a forged counterfeit; and that the people who crafted this letter were 'Abdullāh bin Sabā and his accomplices, not Marwān or anyone else; as for Ḥaḍrat 'Uthmān[ra], his person is far above such an allegation.

CRUELTIES OF THE REBELS UPON THE PEOPLE OF MADINAH

I now return to the series of events, once again. On the basis of this forged letter and due to their pride of having taken control of Madinah, the rebels began to openly perpetrate cruelties. On the one hand, Ḥaḍrat 'Uthmān[ra] was being pressed to step down from *Khilāfat* and on the other hand, the people of Madinah were being harassed so that they would refrain from attempting to help him. The people of Madinah were completely helpless as 2,000 to 3,000 armed soldiers were blockading the streets, junctions and gates of the city. As it was, to fight such an army was not easy, but it was a far-fetched idea to even consider confronting the rebel army in conditions where they would not even allow a few people to gather and it was impossible to collect in groups larger than two or four. Even if a few daring men opted to fight the rebels, this would have resulted in nothing but massacre. The mosque was a place where people could gather. However, the rebels had very cunningly taken measures to prevent this as well. They would spread out in the mosque before prayer and keep the people of Madinah at a distance from one another so that they could not do anything.

ḤAḌRAT 'UTHMĀN[RA] ADMONISHES THE REBELS

Despite this commotion and conflict Ḥaḍrat 'Uthmān[ra] would regularly come to the mosque to lead the prayers. The rebels would not hinder him in this regard and stop him from leading the prayers, until the first Friday approached after their occupation of Madinah. After leading the Friday prayer Ḥaḍrat 'Uthmān[ra] admonished them and said:

> *"O enemies of Islam! Fear God the Exalted. All the people of Madinah know that the Holy Prophet[sa] has cursed you. So repent and erase your sins through deeds of virtue because Allah the Exalted does not erase sins with anything other than good deeds."*

In response Muḥammad bin Maslamah Anṣārī[ra] stood up and said, *"I testify to this fact."* The rebels realised that although their associates thought ill of Ḥaḍrat 'Uthmān[ra], if the companions began to testify in his support and their party learnt that the Holy Prophet[sa] had explicitly made a prophecy about them, then the public may leave them. For this reason they began to stop this practice. The robber Ḥakīm bin Jabalah, who I have mentioned earlier, took hold of Muḥammad bin Maslamah[ra], an intimate Companion of the Holy Prophet[sa] who had stood up in support of *Khilāfat*; not to create any kind of disorder, and forcibly sat him down. Then, Zaid bin Thābit[ra], who had been endowed the magnificent duty of gathering the Holy Quran, stood up in order to testify, but he too was made to sit down by another rebel.[87]

THE REBELS BREAK THE STAFF OF THE HOLY PROPHET[SA]

After this, a member of this party, which professed love for Islam, snatched from Ḥaḍrat 'Uthmān[ra] the staff with which the Holy Prophet[sa] use to take support while delivering the sermon and after him Ḥaḍrat Abū Bakr[ra] and Ḥaḍrat 'Umar[ra] had done the same. He did not stop at this, in fact, he placed this memorabilia of the Holy Prophet[sa], which was a source of thousands of blessings for the Muslim nation, on his knees and broke it. They may have held enmity towards Ḥaḍrat 'Uthmān[ra], they may have harboured hatred for *Khilāfat* but as for the Holy Prophet[sa], they professed love for him! How then did they have the courage to break this memorabilia of the Holy Prophet[sa] with such contempt? Today, Europe has reached the furthest extremity of atheism, but even they still possess a sense that the memorable items left by their elders are to be valued. However, these people, despite claiming to be the followers of Islam, broke

87. Tārīkhuṭ-Ṭabarī, vol. 5, p. 155, Dhikru Masīri Mann Sāra Ilā Dhī Khashabin Min Ahli Miṣra....., Published by Dārul-Fikr, Beirut, 2002 edition [Publishers]

the blessed staff of the Holy Prophet[sa] and tossed it away.[88] This demonstrates that their passion to serve Islam was nothing but mere show; for the leaders of this party were as distant from Islam as the biggest enemies of Islam today.

THE REBELS PELT STONES AT MASJID-E-NABAWĪ AND INJURE ḤAḌRAT 'UTHMĀN[RA]

Even after breaking the staff of the Holy Prophet[sa] the hearts of these rebels were not satisfied. They began to shower stones upon that mosque the foundation of which had been laid by Muḥammad, the Messenger of Allah, may peace and blessings of Allah be upon him, and which had been erected by extremely holy hands. They continued to pelt the companions and the people of Madinah, and drove them out of Masjid-e-Nabawī. They struck Ḥaḍrat 'Uthmān[ra] with so many stones that he fell off the pulpit in a state of unconsciousness and a few men carried him home.[89]

This was the example of the love that these rebels held for Islam and for the bearers of the Islamic shariah. These were the 'high morals' which they desired to establish in the Muslim world by removing Ḥaḍrat 'Uthmān[ra] from *Khilāfat*. After this incident who can say that the party which stood up in

88. Tārīkhuṭ-Ṭabarī, vol. 5, p. 164, Dhikrul-Khabari 'An Qatlihī Wa Kaifa Qutila, Published by Dārul-Fikr, Beirut, 2002 edition [Publishers]

89. Tārīkhuṭ-Ṭabarī, vol. 5, p. 155, Dhikru Masīri Mann Sāra Ilā Dhī Khashabin Min Ahli Miṣra....., Published by Dārul-Fikr, Beirut, 2002 edition [Publishers]

opposition to Ḥaḍrat 'Uthmān[ra] had any connection with the companions, or that in reality, they had been compelled to cause a revolt due to certain measures taken by Ḥaḍrat 'Uthmān[ra], or that their indignation for Islam was the cause of their rage and fury. Their crimes are sufficient to prove that neither did they have any connection with Islam, nor did they hold any love for religion, nor any affection for the companions. They were bent upon ruining the peace and security of the country in order to fulfil their hidden motives and were trying to penetrate the fortress of Islam.

WILLINGNESS OF THE COMPANIONS TO FIGHT THE REBELS

Following this terrible event, the companions and people of Madinah understood that the hearts of the rebels were filled with even greater animosity than what was being displayed. Even though there was not much they could do, some companions, who preferred death over such a state, became intent upon fighting the rebels, come what may. Perhaps, four or five men fighting in opposition to an army of 2,000 or 3,000 men may appear to be madness in the eyes of a worldly person, but as for those who had sacrificed all their possessions for the sake of Islam, it was not burdensome for them whatsoever to fight in its defence. The following companions were also among those who were prepared to fight: Sa'd bin Mālik[ra], Ḥaḍrat Abū Hurairah[ra], Zaid bin Ṣāmit[ra] and Ḥaḍrat Imām Ḥasan[ra]. When this news reached Ḥaḍrat 'Uthmān[ra], he immediately sent them an order instructing them not to fight the rebels under any circumstance and to return to their homes.[90]

The love which Ḥaḍrat 'Uthmān[ra] possessed for the companions of the Holy Prophet[sa] and the *ahl-e-bait,*[91] undoubtedly, prevented a war which was to break out between a few devoted companions and a rebel army of 2,000 to 3,000 men. However, from this event we are able to effectively ascertain the level of passion that was building up among the companions due to the mischief of these rebels. It is only possible for a few men to become willing to stand up against a fierce army if they believe that subservience to it is worse than death. The involvement of Abū Hurairah[ra] and Imām Ḥasan[ra] in this group is especially worthy of attention. Ḥaḍrat Abu Hurairah[ra] was neither a soldier, nor he had performed any military service prior to this in particular. Similarly, even though Ḥaḍrat Imām Ḥasan[ra] was the son of a valiant father and was also brave and courageous himself, he preferred peace and concord, and according to a prophecy of the Holy Prophet[sa], he was a prince of peace.[92] The fact that these two men stood up sword in hand demonstrates that the companions and the other people of Madinah were immensely displeased by the sedition of these rebels.

---

90. Tārīkhuṭ-Ṭabarī, vol. 5, p. 155, Dhikru Masīri Mann Sāra Ilā Dhī Khashabin Min Ahli Miṣra....., Published by Dārul-Fikr, Beirut, 2002 edition [Publishers]
91. Ahl-e-Bait literally means 'people of the house' and refers to the household members of the Holy Prophet[sa].
92. Mustadrak lil-Ḥākam, vol. 3, Kitābu Ma'rifatiṣ-Ṣaḥābah, Bābu Wa Min Faḍā'ilil-Ḥasanibni 'Aliyyibni Abī Ṭālibin, Ḥadīth No. 4809, Published by Dārul-Kutubil-'Ilmiyyah, 1990 edition

THREE MAJOR SUPPORTERS OF THE REBELS IN MADINAH

There were only three residents of Madinah who supported the rebels; one was Muḥammad bin Abī Bakr, who was the son of Ḥaḍrat Abū Bakr[ra]. Historians are of the view that since people showed him respect due to his father, he began to think that he held a position of rank as well. Except for this, neither did he hold any worldly precedence, nor did he benefit from the company of the Holy Prophet[sa], and nor did he gain special religious education afterwards. He was born in the days of *ḥajjatul-wadā'*[93] and was still a suckling baby at the time when the Holy Prophet[sa] passed away. He was only four when Ḥaḍrat Abū Bakr[ra] passed away and was unable to benefit from the upbringing of this exemplary man either.[94]

The second person was Muḥammad bin Abī Ḥudhaifah. He was not from among the companions either. His father had been martyred in the battle of Yamamah and Ḥaḍrat 'Uthmān[ra] had taken his upbringing upon himself. He had nurtured him from childhood. When Ḥaḍrat 'Uthmān[ra] became *Khalīfah*, he asked him for a post but Ḥaḍrat 'Uthmān[ra] refused. He then asked for permission to go out and take up some form work. Ḥaḍrat 'Uthmān[ra] granted him permission, so he went to Egypt. Upon reaching there, he joined the supporters of 'Abdullāh bin Sabā and began inciting people against Ḥaḍrat 'Uthmān[ra]. When the rebels of Egypt attacked Madinah he came along with them.

93. The last hajj performed by the Holy Prophet[sa] prior to his demise, and literally means, 'the farewell hajj.'
94. Tahzībut-Tahzīb, By Ibni Ḥajar 'Asqalānī, vol. 9, p. 80, Muḥammad bin Abī Bakriṣ-Ṣiddīq

However, after having come some distance, he returned, and was not present in Madinah at the time of this conflict.[95]

The third person was 'Ammār bin Yāsir, who was one of the companions. The reason he fell to deception was because he was not very informed in the field of politics. When Ḥaḍrat 'Uthmān[ra] sent him to Egypt so that he could return with a report on the administration of its governor, 'Abdullāh bin Sabā welcomed him and turned him against the governor of Egypt. Moreover, since the governor had bitterly opposed the Holy Prophet[sa] in his days of disbelief and had accepted Islam after the victory of Makkah, 'Ammār bin Yāsir was quickly ensnared by them. After creating suspicion against the governor, 'Abdullāh bin Sabā slowly made him suspicious of Ḥaḍrat 'Uthmān[ra] as well.[96] However, 'Ammār bin Yāsir did not practically participate in the rebellion. Although he was present in Madinah when it was attacked, apart from sitting quietly at home and not taking part in opposing the rebels, practically, he did not take any part in the rebellion. He was completely innocent of the crimes committed by the rebels.

ḤAḌRAT 'UTHMĀN[RA] IS ASKED TO STEP DOWN FROM KHILĀFAT

Besides these three, no one in Madinah – be it a Companion[ra] or anyone else – held sympathy for the rebels.

95. Tārīkhuṭ-Ṭabarī, vol. 5, pp. 186-187, Dhikru Ba'di Siyari Uthmān....., Published by Dārul-Fikr, Beirut, 2002 edition

96. Tārīkhuṭ-Ṭabarī, vol. 5, p. 148, Dhikru Masīri Mann Sāra Ilā Dhī Khashabin Min Ahli Miṣra....., Published by Dārul-Fikr, Beirut, 2002 edition [Publishers]

Everyone would send curse upon the rebels and reproach them, but they did not care, because all the power was in their hands at the time. For up to twenty days the rebels tried to convince Ḥaḍrat ‘Uthmān[ra] to somehow step down from *Khilāfat* through dialogue alone. However, Ḥaḍrat ‘Uthmān[ra] plainly refused and said:

> *"Neither can I remove the garment which God the Exalted, has clothed me with, nor can I leave the people of Muḥammad[sa] unsheltered so that anyone who wishes may oppress another."*[97]

Ḥaḍrat ‘Uthmān[ra] continued to admonish the rebels to refrain from creating conflict and went on to say:

> *"Today these people create disorder and detest my very existence. But when I shall be no more, they shall wish, 'If only each and every day of the life of ‘Uthmān[ra] was transformed into one year each and would that he had not departed from us so soon.' For after me there shall be severe bloodshed, rights shall be violated and governance shall take a completely different turn."*

(As such, in the Banū Umayyah period, *khilāfat* was replaced by secular rule and these rebels were given such harsh punishments that they forgot all their mischief).

97. Tārīkhuṭ-Ṭabarī, vol. 5, p. 180, Dhikrul-Khabari ‘An Qatlihī Wa Kaifa Qutila, Published by Dārul-Fikr, Beirut, 2002 edition

THE HOUSE OF ḤAḌRAT 'UTHMĀN[RA] BESIEGED

After twenty days had elapsed, the rebels thought that a quick decision was required, lest the armies from the surrounding provinces arrive and they were made to suffer the consequences of their actions. For this reason they stopped Ḥaḍrat 'Uthmān[ra] from leaving his house, and also forbade the transfer of food and drink into his house. They thought that perhaps in this manner, Ḥaḍrat 'Uthmān[ra] would be compelled to accept their demands.

The administration of Madinah was now in their hands. The three armies collectively accepted Ghāfiqī, the commander of the Egyptian armies, as their commander in chief. So, it was as if, Ghāfiqī was the ruler of Madinah at the time; Ashtar commanded the army of Kufah and Ḥakīm bin Jabalah (the same robber who had been imprisoned in Basrah, on the order of Ḥaḍrat 'Uthmān[ra], for robbing the wealth of non-Muslim subjects) commanded the army of Basrah, under the leadership of Ghāfiqī. Once again, this proves that the rebels of Egypt were the root cause of this conflict, where 'Abdullāh bin Sabā was at work. Ghāfiqī would lead the prayers in *Masjid-e-Nabawī* while the companions of the Holy Prophet[sa] would either remain locked up in their homes or would be compelled to offer prayers behind him.[98]

The rebels did not cause people much hindrance until

---

98. Tārīkhuṭ-Ṭabarī, vol. 5, pp. 155-156, Dhikru Masīri Mann Sāra Ilā Dhī Khashabin Min Ahli Miṣra..... / p. 172, Dhikrul-Khabari 'An Qatlihī Wa Kaifa Qutila, Published by Dārul-Fikr, Beirut, 2002 edition [Publishers]

they decided to lay siege upon the house of Ḥaḍrat 'Uthmān[ra]. However, as soon as they laid siege [upon his house], they began to oppress other people as well. Instead of being *Dārul-Amn* [the House of Peace], Madinah had now become *Dārul-Ḥarb* [the House of War]. The respect and honour of the people of Madinah was in danger; no one would step out of his house unarmed and the rebels would kill anyone who confronted them.

ḤAḌRAT 'ALĪ[RA] ADMONISHES THE BESIEGERS

When the rebels had surrounded Ḥaḍrat 'Uthmān[ra] and even went so far as to stop water from entering [his house], he sent a neighbour's son to Ḥaḍrat 'Alī[ra], Ḥaḍrat Ṭalḥah[ra], Ḥaḍrat Zubair[ra] and the *ummahātul-mu'minīn*[99] for assistance saying, *"The rebels have even cut our water supply. If you are able to do something, then please arrange for water to be conveyed to us."* From among the men, Ḥaḍrat 'Alī[ra] was the first to arrive. He admonished the rebels saying:

> *"What sort of a behaviour have you adopted? Your actions neither resemble those of the believers nor the disbelievers. Do not prevent food and drink from entering the house of Ḥaḍrat 'Uthmān[ra]. Even the Romans and Persians provide their prisoners with food and water. According to the Islamic practice your conduct is not acceptable in the least. Besides, what harm has Ḥaḍrat 'Uthmān[ra] done to you that you deem it permissible to imprison him and kill him?"*

---

99. A title for the wives of the Holy Prophetsa and literally means, 'the mothers of the believers.' [Publishers]

This admonition of Ḥaḍrat 'Alī[ra] had no influence on them whatsoever. They plainly said, *"Whatever the case may be, we shall not allow food or water to reach him."* This was the reply the rebels gave to the person who they deemed to be the *waṣī* of the Holy Prophet[sa] and his true successor. After this reply, does the need for any other testimony remain in order to prove that this party, who declared Ḥaḍrat 'Alī[ra] to be the *waṣī*, had not left their homes in support of the truth or out of their love for the *ahl-e-bait*; rather, only to fulfil their base desires?

TREATMENT OF THE REBELS TOWARDS ḤAḌRAT UMMI ḤABĪBAH[RA]

From among the *ummahātul-mu'minīn*, Ḥaḍrat Ummi Ḥabībah[ra] was the first to come to the aid of Ḥaḍrat 'Uthmān[ra]. Mounted on a mule, she brought a water-skin along with her. However, her real objective was to safeguard all the wills of the orphans and widows that belonged to Banū Umayyah, which were in the possession of Ḥaḍrat 'Uthmān[ra]. When she saw that the rebels had stopped the water supply of Ḥaḍrat 'Uthmān[ra], she became fearful that they might destroy these wills as well, and thus desired to somehow safeguard these documents. After all, there were other means by which she could have delivered the water. When Ḥaḍrat Ummi Ḥabībah reached the door of Ḥaḍrat 'Uthmān[ra], just as the rebels were about to stop her, the people exclaimed, *"This is Ummul-Mu'minīn, Ummi Ḥabībah[ra]."* However, the rebels still persisted and started beating her mule. *Ummul-Mu'minīn*, Ummi Ḥabībah[ra] explained:

"I fear lest the wills of the orphans and widows of the Banū

Umayyah should be destroyed. For this reason, I wish to go inside in order to arrange for their safekeeping."

However, these wretched people replied to the blessed wife of the Holy Prophet[sa], *"You are lying."* The rebels then attacked her mule and cut the straps of its packsaddle. The saddle fell to one side. Ḥaḍrat Ummi Ḥabībah[ra] was on the verge of falling off and being martyred under the feet of the rebels, but a few people of Madinah, who were close by, dashed to her aid and escorted her home.[100]

AN EXAMPLE OF THE RELIGIOUS INDIGNATION OF ḤAḌRAT UMMI ḤABĪBAH[RA]

This was the treatment which they meted out to the blessed wife of the Holy Prophet[sa]. Ḥaḍrat Ummi Ḥabībah[ra] possessed such profound loyalty and love for the Holy Prophet[sa] that after a separation of about fifteen to sixteen years, when her father, who was the chief of Arabia and held the position of a king in Makkah came to Madinah on a special political mission and came to meet her, she pulled away the bedding of the Holy Prophet[sa] from beneath him. This was because she could not bear to see the pure cloth of the Messenger of Allah touch the impure body of an idolater. It is surprising that in the absence of Muḥammad[sa], the Messenger of Allah, Ḥaḍrat Ummi Ḥabībah[ra] safeguarded the sanctity of even his cloth,[101] whereas these rebels did not even show veneration to the revered

100. Tārīkhuṭ-Ṭabarī, vol. 5, p. 177, Dhikrul-Khabari 'An Qatlihī Wa Kaifa Qutila, Published by Dārul-Fikr, Beirut, 2002 edition

101. Iṣābatu Fī Tamīziṣ-Ṣaḥābah, vol. 8, p. 142, Ramlah Bintu Abī Sufyān, Dārul-Kutubil-'Ilmiyyah, Beirut, 2005 edition [Publishers]

wife of Muḥammad[sa], the Messenger of Allah, in his absence. These foolish people said that the wife of the Holy Prophet[sa] was a liar, even though she was correct in her statement. Ḥaḍrat 'Uthmān[ra] was the guardian of the orphans of Banū Umayyah. On seeing their growing enmity, her concern that the wealth of the orphans and widows may go to waste was correct. The true liars were those who took up the task of destroying the faith whilst claiming to love Muḥammad[sa], the Messenger of Allah; not Ummi Ḥabībah[ra], *Ummul-Mu'minīn.*[102]

ḤAḌRAT 'Ā'ISHAH[RA] PREPARES FOR HAJJ

When news of the treatment meted out to Ḥaḍrat Ummi Ḥabībah[ra] spread throughout Madinah, the companions and residents of Madinah were left shocked; they understood that now it was useless to hope of any good to come from the rebels. It was at this very time that Ḥaḍrat 'Ā'ishah[ra] decided to go for hajj and she began to make preparations for the journey. When people learned that she was about to leave Madinah, some of them requested that if she remained behind, perhaps this would be conducive to bringing an end to the conflict and the rebels would take heed. However, she refused saying:

> *"Do you want me to receive the same treatment as Ummi Ḥabībah[ra]. By God! I cannot put my honour at risk (as she was the honour of the Holy Prophet[sa]). If I am targeted in any way, what will be the means of my protection? Only*

102. Tārīkhuṭ-Ṭabarī, vol. 5, pp. 177-178, Dhikrul-Khabari 'An Qatlihī Wa Kaifa Qutila, Published by Dārul-Fikr, Beirut, 2002 edition

God knows the extent to which the rebels will grow in their mischief and what will be their outcome."

Just as Ḥaḍrat 'Ā'ishah Ṣiddīqah[ra] was leaving she devised a strategy; had it succeeded, this conflict may have been suppressed to some extent. She sent a message to her brother, Muḥammad bin Abī Bakr, that he should also accompany her to perform hajj but he refused. Upon this, Ḥaḍrat 'Ā'ishah[ra] said, *"What am I to do, I am helpless. If I had the strength, I would never allow these rebels to succeed in their designs."*

ḤAḌRAT 'UTHMĀN[RA] SENDS A CIRCULAR TO THE PROVINCIAL GOVERNORS

Ḥaḍrat 'Ā'ishah[ra] had gone for hajj and some companions, who were able to leave Madinah, also left. The remaining people except for a few prominent companions remained in their homes. Ultimately, even Ḥaḍrat 'Uthmān[ra] felt that the rebels would not settle through leniency and he dispatched a letter to all the provincial governors, the summary of which is as follows:

"After Ḥaḍrat Abū Bakr[ra] and Ḥaḍrat 'Umar[ra], without any desire or request of my own, I was included among those who were entrusted the duty of holding counsel regarding Khilāfat. Then, I was elected to the office of Khilāfat without any desire or request of my own. Without fail, I continued the works which the previous Khulafā'[ra] undertook and I did not introduce any innovations in the faith of my own accord. However, the seed of evil was planted into the hearts of certain people, mischief arose and then they began to plot against me; they expressed one

thing before the people, while concealing another thing in their hearts. These people began to level such accusations against me as were levelled against the Khulafā'[ra] *before me as well. However, I remained silent despite knowing of this. Taking advantage of my mercy, these people grew even more in their mischief. Ultimately, they attacked Madinah in the likeness of disbelievers. So, if there is anything you can do then please arrange for some help."*[103]

Similarly, a few days later, Ḥaḍrat 'Uthmān[ra] wrote a letter to the people who had come to perform hajj. The gist of [this letter] is set out below.

A LETTER TO THE PILGRIMS FROM ḤAḌRAT 'UTHMĀN[RA]

"I draw your attention towards God the Exalted and remind you of His favours. At this time certain people are creating mischief and are engaged in attempts to cause divide in Islam. However, these people have not even taken into consideration that God appoints the Khalīfah, just as He says:

وَعَدَ اللّٰهُ الَّذِيْنَ اٰمَنُوْا مِنْكُمْ وَعَمِلُوا الصّٰلِحٰتِ لَيَسْتَخْلِفَنَّهُمْ فِي الْاَرْضِ

[meaning, Allah has promised to those among you who

103. Tārīkhuṭ-Ṭabarī, vol. 5, p. 154, Dhikru Masīri Mann Sāra Ilā Dhī Khashabin Min Ahli Miṣra....., Published by Dārul-Fikr, Beirut, 2002 edition [Publishers]

believe and do good works that He will surely make them Successors in the earth].[104]

Moreover, they did not value [the importance of] unity, even though God the Exalted has commanded:

وَاعۡتَصِمُوۡا بِحَبۡلِ اللّٰهِ جَمِيۡعًا

[meaning, and hold fast all together by the rope of Allah].[105]

Furthermore, they accepted the words of those who accused me and did not pay heed to this command of the Holy Quran:

يٰۤاَيُّهَا الَّذِيۡنَ اٰمَنُوۡۤا اِنۡ جَآءَكُمۡ فَاسِقٌۢ بِنَبَاٍ فَتَبَيَّنُوۡۤا

[meaning, O ye who believe! if an unrighteous person brings you any news, ascertain the correctness of the report fully].[106]

They did not honour their bai'at to me, even though Allah the Exalted says with relation to the Holy Prophet[sa]:

اِنَّ الَّذِيۡنَ يُبَايِعُوۡنَكَ اِنَّمَا يُبَايِعُوۡنَ اللّٰهَ ؕ

[meaning, verily, those who swear allegiance to thee indeed swear allegiance to Allah].[107]

And I am a successor of the Noble Messenger[sa]. No nation can progress without a leader and if there is no Imām then the community is destined to be ruined and destroyed.

104. An-Nūr (24:56)
105. Āl-e-'Imrān (3:104)
106. Al-Ḥujurāt (49:7)
107. Al-Fatḥ (48:11)

These people desire to destroy and ruin the Muslim ummah; this is their only objective because I accepted their wish and promised to change [various] governors but despite this, they did not seize making mischief. Now, they demand one out of three things. Firstly, they demand that revenge should be sought from me for all those people who have received punished in my reign. If I do not agree, then I should step down from Khilāfat and they will appoint someone else in my place. If I do not agree to this either, then they threaten that they will send a message to all their supporters to no longer be obedient to me. The answer with respect to the first demand is that the Khulafā'[ra] *before me also committed judgmental errors but they were never punished. Furthermore, what other motive besides killing me can there be in imposing so many punishments upon me.*

As for my deposition from Khilāfat, my reply is that if these people tear my flesh into bits with pincers, I can accept this, but I cannot step down from Khilāfat.

Now remains the third point, i.e., [if I do not agree to the above], they will send their men in all directions telling people not to obey me. For this, I am not held responsible by God if they wish to act in violation of the shariah. Even before, when they pledged allegiance to me, I did not compel them. Neither I, nor God the Exalted is pleased with the action of anyone who wishes to break his covenant. Of course, such a person may do as he wishes on his own accord."[108]

Since the days of hajj were fast approaching and people were converging upon *Makkah Mukarramah* from all corners, Ḥaḍrat 'Uthmān[ra] appointed Ḥaḍrat 'Abdullāh bin 'Abbās[ra] and dispatched him as the Amir for hajj lest the rebels created disorder there as well. This way Ḥaḍrat 'Abdullāh bin 'Abbās[ra] could also urge the Muslims gathering for hajj to assist the people of Madinah. Even Ḥaḍrat 'Abdullāh bin 'Abbās[ra] submitted, *"I would prefer to do jihad against these people."* However, Ḥaḍrat 'Uthmān[ra] compelled him to go for hajj and discharge his duties as the Amir for hajj, in order to prevent the rebels from spreading their mischief there and also to urge the pilgrims gathering there to help the people of Madinah. The above-mentioned letter of Ḥaḍrat 'Uthmān[ra] was sent along with him as well. When the rebels learned of these letters they grew in their violence. They began to look for an excuse to fight so that they could martyr Ḥaḍrat 'Uthmān[ra]. All their efforts, however, were in vain and Ḥaḍrat 'Uthmān[ra] would not give them an opportunity to make mischief.

THE REBELS PELT STONES AT THE HOUSE OF ḤAḌRAT 'UTHMĀN[RA]

In the end, out of frustration, the scheme devised by the rebels was that they would stone the house of Ḥaḍrat 'Uthmān[ra] at night fall when everyone would fall asleep. In this manner,

108. Tārīkhuṭ-Ṭabarī, vol. 5, pp. 192-193, Dhikrul-Khabari 'Anis-Sababilladhī Min Ajlihī, Published by Dārul-Fikr, Beirut, 2002 edition [Publishers]

they would provoke the members of the household so that they too would throw stones in retaliation; so the rebels could say that they [the household of Ḥaḍrat 'Uthmān[ra]] initiated the attack and they were compelled to respond. However, Ḥaḍrat 'Uthmān[ra] had prohibited all the members of his household from retaliating. One day, upon finding an opportunity, he approached the wall and said:

> *'O people! In your view I am a sinner, but what wrong have the others committed? When you throw stones there is also a risk of others being injured.'*

The rebels plainly denied and said that they had not thrown any stones. Ḥaḍrat 'Uthmān[ra] said, *"If you do not throw them, then who does?"* The rebels replied, *"God the Exalted probably throws them."*

نَعُوْذُ بِاللّٰہِ مِنْ ذَالِکَ ۔[109]

To this, Ḥaḍrat 'Uthmān[ra] responded:

> *'You speak lies! If God the Exalted had thrown stones at us, then not one of His stones would have missed; but the stones thrown by you fall off target as well.'*[110]

After saying this, Ḥaḍrat 'Uthmān[ra] left them to their work.

109. We seek refuge with Allah from such a thing. [Publishers]

110. Tārīkhuṭ-Ṭabarī, vol. 5, p. 177, Dhikrul-Khabari 'An Qatlihī Wa Kaifa Qutila, Published by Dārul-Fikr, Beirut, 2002 edition [Publishers]

WORTHY EFFORTS OF THE COMPANIONS IN SUPPRESSING THE DISORDER

Although the companions were no longer given a chance to gather in the company of Ḥaḍrat 'Uthmānra, even still, they were not negligent of their duty. They had divided their work into two parts as a wise measure at the time. Those men who were elderly and who due to their morals, possessed a great influence on the public, spent their time admonishing the rebels; as for those people who possessed no such influence, or were young, would remain engaged in efforts to protect Ḥaḍrat 'Uthmānra.

From among the former group, Ḥaḍrat 'Alīra and Ḥaḍrat Sa'd bin Waqqāṣra, the conqueror of Persia, strove the hardest to suppress the conflict. Ḥaḍrat 'Alīra had especially devoted his time to this cause, leaving aside all his other work. As such, a person by the name of 'Abdur-Raḥmān, who was an eye witness of these events, says:

> *"In the days of disorder, I saw that Ḥaḍrat 'Alīra had abandoned all his work. Day and night, he would remain concerned about how he could calm the temper of the enemies of Ḥaḍrat 'Uthmānra and bring an end to his sufferings. On one occasion, when there was a delay in conveying water to Ḥaḍrat 'Uthmānra, he became very displeased with Ḥaḍrat Ṭalḥahra to whom this task was assigned. Ḥaḍrat 'Alīra did not rest until water had reached the home of Ḥaḍrat 'Uthmānra."*

In ones and twos, whenever they could find an opportunity, the second group began to gather in the house of Ḥaḍrat 'Uthmānra or in neighbouring houses. This party had firmly resolved that they would give their lives but not let Ḥaḍrat 'Uthmānra come in harm's way. Besides the children of Ḥaḍrat 'Alīra, Ḥaḍrat Ṭalḥahra and Ḥaḍrat Zubairra, even a party of the companions themselves was a part of this group. These men guarded the house of Ḥaḍrat 'Uthmānra, day and night, and would not allow any enemy to reach Ḥaḍrat 'Uthmānra. Although this small party could not stand up to such a large army, but since the rebels were after an excuse to kill Ḥaḍrat 'Uthmānra, they would not put up much of a resistance either. The events of that time shed such light upon the level of devotion Ḥaḍrat 'Uthmānra possessed for the welfare of Islam that one is left astonished. An army of three thousand strong stood at his door and no strategy to save himself was devised. He even stopped those who endeavoured to save him saying, *"Leave! Do not put your lives in danger. These people only hold enmity for me; they have no objection against you."* His eye could foresee the time when Islam would be in grave danger at the hands of these rebels; not only apparent unity, but even the spiritual administration would reach the verge of falling apart. Ḥaḍrat 'Uthmānra knew that at that time each and every Companionra would be required for the protection and establishment of Islam. For this reason, he did not want the companions to lose their lives in a futile attempt to save his life and continued advising all of them not to withstand the rebels. He desired that insofar as possible, the community which had benefited from the company of the Messenger of Allah, should be safeguarded, in order to dispel disorders which were to arise in the future. Despite his instructions, however, the companions who would happen to find an opportunity to reach the house of Ḥaḍrat 'Uthmānra did not fail in fulfilling their obligation. They gave precedence to the danger at hand over such dangers that were yet to come. If the lives [of the companions] were secure at the time, then it was only because the rebels felt no need to hurry and were on the lookout for an excuse [to murder Ḥaḍrat ʻUthmān[ra]]. Ultimately, however, the hour arrived when it became impossible to wait any longer, because the heart-rendering message of Ḥaḍrat ʻUthmān[ra], which he had sent to the Muslims who were gathering for hajj, had now been read out before the crowd of pilgrims. The valley of Makkah echoed this voice from one end to another. The Muslim pilgrims had decided that after the hajj, they would not remain deprived of gaining the spiritual reward of performing jihad as well; they would uproot the rebels of Egypt and their associates. Rebel spies had informed their people of this intention and now signs of agitation began to arise in their camp. This was to such extent that murmurings within the rebel camp began to take place suggesting that now there was no other option but to kill this man; if they did not kill him, there would be no uncertainty in their own massacre at the hands of the Muslims.

This anxiety was further intensified by the news that the letters of Ḥaḍrat ʻUthmān[ra] had now reached Syria, Kufah and Basrah as well, and the people there, who were already waiting for the orders of Ḥaḍrat ʻUthmān[ra], had been further enraged upon the receipt of these letters. Not to mention that taking it upon themselves, the companions had drawn the attention of all the Muslims towards their obligations in mosques and gatherings, and they had issued the verdict of performing jihad against the rebels. The companions said, *"A person, who does not perform jihad on this day, is as if he has done nothing."* If in Kufah 'Uqbah bin 'Amr[ra], 'Abdullāh bin Abī Aufā[ra], Ḥanẓalah bin Rabī' At-Tamīmī[ra] and other noble companions had roused the people into supporting the people of Madinah, then 'Imrān bin Ḥaṣīn[ra], Anas bin Mālik[ra], Hishām bin 'Āmir[ra] and other companions had done the same in Basrah. If in Syria 'Ubādah bin Ṣāmit[ra], Abū Umāmah[111] and other companions had motivated the people to answer to the call of Ḥaḍrat 'Uthmān[ra] then Khārijah and others had done the same in Egypt. Armies from every province were joining forces and marching towards Madinah.[112]

THE REBELS ATTACK THE HOUSE OFḤAḌRAT 'UTHMĀN[RA]

Hence, this news intensified the anxiety of the rebels. Finally, they attacked the house of Ḥaḍrat 'Uthmān[ra] and sought to forcefully enter. The companions confronted them and a fierce battle ensued. Although the companions were few in number, their religions indignation was covering for this disadvantage. Since the area where this battle took place, i.e., in front of the house of Ḥaḍrat 'Uthmān[ra] was narrow, due to this

111. According to the narration of Ṭabarī, Ḥaḍrat Abū Dardā' Anṣārī was also among those companions who urged people to support Ḥaḍrat 'Uthmān[ra] in Syria. However, it appears from other narrations that he had already passed away prior to the martyrdom of Ḥaḍrat 'Uthmān[ra], as established by Istī'āb and Iṣābah. This is correct, however, as mentioned earlier, during his lifetime, he too endeavoured to wipe out this conflict.

112. Tārīkhuṭ-Ṭabarī, vol. 5, p. 154-155, Dhikru Masīri Mann Sāra Ilā Dhī Khashabin Min Ahli Miṣra....., Published by Dārul-Fikr, Beirut, 2002 edition

reason as well, the rebels were unable to exploit their advantage in number. When Ḥaḍrat 'Uthmān[ra] learned of this battle he forbade the companions from fighting. However, at that time, they viewed abandoning Ḥaḍrat 'Uthmān[ra] to be against honesty and contrary to the teaching of obedience. Hence, they refused to return despite Ḥaḍrat 'Uthmān[ra] appealing to them in the name of God.

ḤAḌRAT 'UTHMĀN[RA] ORDERS THE COMPANIONS

In the end, Ḥaḍrat 'Uthmān[ra] took a shield in his hand, came out and lead the companions inside his house. He then had the doors closed and enjoined the companions and their helpers:

> *"God the Exalted has not given you the world so that you may incline towards it. In fact, he has granted you the world so that by this means, you may gather provisions for the hereafter. So, let not that which is to perish make you unmindful. Give precedence to that which shall remain over that which is to perish. Be mindful of you meeting with God the Exalted and do not allow your community to disperse. Do not forget the Divine favour that you were on the brink of a pit of destruction and God the Exalted saved you out of His bounty and made you as brothers."*

Having said this he dismissed them and said:

> *"May God the Exalted be your Guardian and Helper. All of you leave the house now, and call for those companions who have been barred from reaching me, especially Ḥaḍrat 'Alī[ra], Ḥaḍrat Ṭalḥah[ra] and Ḥaḍrat Zubair[ra]."*

These people stepped out and the other companions were also

called. At the time, such a mood was developing and such a degree of sorrow was overshadowing the atmosphere, that even the rebels could not remain unaffected. And why would this not be the case? Everyone was observing that a candle lit by Muḥammad[sa], the Messenger of Allah, upon completing its life in the world was now about to disappear from the eyes of the people. Therefore, the rebels did not cause much hindrance and all the companions gathered. When everyone had come together, Ḥaḍrat 'Uthmān[ra] climbed the wall of his house and said, *"Come close to me."* When they had all come close to him, Ḥaḍrat 'Uthmān[ra] said, *"O people! Sit down."* At this, the companions sat down and inspired by the awe of the gathering, so did the rebels. When they had all sat down Ḥaḍrat 'Uthmān[ra] said:

> *"People of Madinah! I entrust you to God the Exalted and pray to Him that after me, He may arrange for a better successor than me. After today, until God the Exalted issues a decree in my regard, I shall not step out of my house and I shall not pass on authority to anyone by which he may rule over you in terms of religion or worldly rule. I leave it to God the Exalted to choose whoever He desires for His work."*

After this he appealed in the name of Allah to the companions and the other people of Madinah, not to put their own lives in grave danger by protecting him and to go to their homes.

This instruction of Ḥaḍrat 'Uthmān[ra] created a serious disagreement among the companions, a disagreement the likes of which cannot be found prior to this. The companions knew nothing but to obey every command, but today, in obeying this instruction, some perceived the stench of treachery, as opposed to obedience. Some companions gave precedence to the aspect of obedience and unwillingly did away with their intention of fighting the rebels from then on. Perhaps they thought that their duty was only to be obedient and it was not their task to reflect upon the results that would come about by obeying this command. However, some companions refused to obey this order, because although they knew that it was an obligation to obey the *Khalīfah*, but if the *Khalīfah* commands people to abandon him, this effectively means that they should sever their ties with *Khilāfat*; hence, this kind of obedience actually results in treachery. Furthermore, they also knew that Ḥaḍrat 'Uthmān[ra] was sending them home in order to protect their lives. How then, could they leave such a loving person in danger and go to their homes? All the prominent companions were among the latter group. As such, despite this command, the sons of Ḥaḍrat 'Alī[ra], Ḥaḍrat Ṭalḥah[ra] and Ḥaḍrat Zubair[ra], under the order of their respective fathers, constantly stood guard at the porch of Ḥaḍrat 'Uthmān[ra] and did not put their swords into their sheaths.[113]

ANXIETY OF THE REBELS UPON THE RETURN OF THE PILGRIMS

The anxiety and ebullition of the rebels knew no bounds when the odd one or two people – who were returning after having completed hajj – began to enter Madinah; they were

---

113. Tārīkhuṭ-Ṭabarī, vol. 5, pp. 176-179, Dhikrul-Khabari 'An Qatlihī Wa Kaifa Qutila, Published by Dārul-Fikr, Beirut, 2002 edition [Publishers]

certain that now the time for their judgement had drawn very close. After performing hajj, Mughīrah bin Al-Akhnas was the first person who entered Madinah in order to gain the spiritual reward of jihad. As soon as he arrived, the rebels received news that the army of Basrah, which was coming to help the Muslims, had reached Ṣirār, which was only at a journey of one day from Madinah. Overwhelmed by this news, the rebels decided that it was now vital that they fulfil their objective at all costs. Those companions and their friends who had refused to relinquish their protection of Ḥaḍrat 'Uthmān[ra] despite his prohibition and those who had plainly said, *"How will we face God the Exalted if we desert you despite having the strength in our arms to fight?"* were now standing guard from inside the house due to their small number. Hence, it was not difficult for the rebels to reach the door. The rebels collected piles of wood outside the door and set light to them, so that the door would burn down and they could find an entrance into [the house]. Upon observing this, the companions deemed it inappropriate to remain inside and they desired to step out swords in hand. However, Ḥaḍrat 'Uthmān[ra] stopped them from doing so and said:

> *"What more can there be than setting the house on fire? Whatever was to happen has now happened. Do not put your lives in danger and return to your homes. These people only harbour enmity against myself, but soon, they shall be remorseful for their doing. I absolve every person*

of his duty who is obliged to obey me and give up my right upon him."[114]

However, the companions as well as others did not accept this and stepped out swords in hand. As they were coming out, Ḥaḍrat Abu Hurairah[ra] arrived as well and joined them even though he was not the kind of person to engage in battle. Abū Hurairah[ra] said, *"What battle can be superior to the battle of this day?"*

Then he looked towards the rebels and said:

وَيٰقَوۡمِ مَا لِيۡۤ اَدۡعُوۡكُمۡ اِلَى النَّجٰوةِ وَتَدۡعُوۡنَنِيۡۤ اِلَى النَّارِ

"O my people, why is it that I call you towards salvation and you call me towards the Fire."

THE COMPANIONS FIGHT THE REBELS

This battle was an exceptional one. A hand full of companions who were able to gather at the time fought desperately against this grand army. On that day, even Ḥaḍrat Imām Ḥasan[ra], who was extremely peace loving, in fact, he was a prince of peace, attacked the enemy and would recite *rajaz.*[115] The couplets recited by Ḥaḍrat Imām Ḥasan and Muḥammad bin Ṭalḥah on that day are especially worthy of mention because

114. Tārīkhuṭ-Ṭabarī, vol. 5, p. 175-179/183, Dhikrul-Khabari 'An Qatlihī Wa Kaifa Qutila, Published by Dārul-Fikr, Beirut, 2002 edition

115. A specific meter in Arabic poetry, which contains a discourse in rhyme. This word also denotes the recitation of poetic verses in general. [Publishers]

they provide a deep understanding of their heartfelt feelings at the time.

Ḥaḍrat Imām Ḥasan[ra] would recite the following couplet and attack the rebels:

لَا دِيْنُهُمْ دِيْنِى وَلَا اَنَا مِنْهُمْ حَتّٰى اَسِيْرَ اِلىٰ طَمَارِ شَمَام

"Their faith is not my faith nor do I have any relation with them; I shall fight them until I reach the summit of mount Shamām."[116]

Shamām is a mountain in Arabia which serves as a similitude for conquering heights and the achievement of one's goal. Ḥaḍrat Imām Ḥasan[ra] meant to say that he would continue to fight the rebels until he attained his objective and would not make peace with them, because the disagreement between both parties was not a trivial one, whereby [the believers] could develop a relationship with them, without having conquered them. These were the thoughts that were billowing in the heart of this prince of peace. Let us now take the *rajaz* of the son of Ṭalḥah[ra], who says:

اَنَا ابْنُ مَنْ حَامىٰ عَلَيْهِ بِاُحَد وَرَدَّ اَحْزَابا علىٰ رَغْم مَعَد

"I am the son of he who protected the Holy Prophet[sa] on the day of Uḥad and defeated the Arabs despite their full efforts."

In other words, this day was also similar to the day of Uḥad; just as his father had offered his hand to be pierced with arrows but

116. Tārīkhuṭ-Ṭabarī, vol. 5, p. 179, Dhikrul-Khabari 'An Qatlihī Wa Kaifa Qutila, Published by Dārul-Fikr, Beirut, 2002 edition

did not let any harm come to the Holy Prophet[sa], he would do the same.

Ḥaḍrat 'Abdullāh bin Zubair[ra] also participated in this battle and was badly injured. Marwān also sustained serious injuries and barely escaped the clutches of death. Mughīrah bin Al-Akhnas was killed. When the person who had attacked Mughīrah saw that not only had he been wounded but that he had been killed, he exclaimed:

إِنَّا لِلّٰهِ وَإِنَّآ إِلَيْهِ رٰجِعُوْنَ

[meaning, surely, to Allah we belong and to Him shall we return].[117]

The chief of the army reprimanded him saying, *"You express regret on an occasion of happiness!"* He replied:

> *"Last night I saw in a dream that a person said, 'Give news of hell to the killer of Mughīrah.' So upon learning that I am his killer I was bound to be shocked by this."*[118]

Besides the above mentioned people others were also injured and killed; the party protecting Ḥaḍrat 'Uthmān[ra] became even smaller. If on the one hand, the rebels persisted in their obstinacy despite a heavenly warning and continued to fight against the beloved party of God the Exalted, then on the other hand, the devotees also did not slacken in setting an excellent example of faith. Despite the fact that most guards had

---

117. Al-Baqarah (2:157) [Publishers]

118. Tārīkhuṭ-Ṭabarī, vol. 5, p. 179-180, Dhikrul-Khabari 'An Qatlihī Wa Kaifa Qutila, Published by Dārul-Fikr, Beirut, 2002 edition [Publishers]

been killed or injured, a small party continued to guard the door without fail.

Since the rebels had apparently gained victory already, they sent someone to Ḥaḍrat 'Uthmān[ra] again, as a final strategy, to have him resign from *Khilāfat*. They felt that if he resigned himself then the Muslims would have no authority or opportunity to punish the rebels. When the messenger reached Ḥaḍrat 'Uthmān[ra], he said:

> *"I have refrained from vices even in the days of jahiliyyah and have not violated the injunctions [of God] after accepting Islam. Why and for what crime should I leave the office which God the Exalted has conferred upon me? I shall never remove the garment which God the Exalted has clothed me with."*

The messenger returned after hearing this reply and addressed his people in the following words:

> *"By God! We have fallen into grave trial. By God! We cannot escape the clutches of the Muslims without killing 'Uthmān[ra] (because in this case the government would topple and its administration would crumble and there would be no one to question them) but killing him is in no way permissible."*[119]

Not only do the words of this person highlight the anxiety of the rebels, but they also establish that Ḥaḍrat 'Uthmān[ra] had still not allowed anything to arise which the rebels could have used as an excuse. In their hearts, the rebels

119. Tārīkhuṭ-Ṭabarī, vol. 5, pp. 178-180, Dhikrul-Khabari 'An Qatlihī Wa Kaifa Qutila, Published by Dārul-Fikr, Beirut, 2002 edition [Publishers]

knew that killing Ḥaḍrat 'Uthmān[ra] was not lawful under any circumstances.

'ABDULLĀH[RA] BIN SALĀM ADMONISHES THE REBELS

Ḥaḍrat 'Abdullāh[ra] bin Salām arrived when the rebels were plotting to assassinate Ḥaḍrat 'Uthmān[ra]. Ḥaḍrat 'Abdullāh[ra] bin Salām was greatly revered within his tribe even when he was a disbeliever and the Jews believed him to be their chief and a peerless scholar. He stood at the door and began to admonish the rebels, and he forbade them from killing Ḥaḍrat 'Uthmān[ra] saying:

> *"O People! Do not draw the sword of God up your heads. By God! If you draw the sword you will never find an opportunity to put it back into its sheath; conflict and discord among the Muslims shall never end. Pay heed! Today, the government [punishes criminals] by the whip (generally lashing is the penalty for a criminal offence in the Islamic penal code), but if you kill this man, then the State will not be able to maintain order without the sword (i.e. people will be killed for petty crimes)*[120]. *Keep in mind that the angels are the guardians of Madinah at this time; if you kill him, the angels will desert Madinah."*

The benefit that the rebels derived from this admonition was

---

120. In other words, rebels such as these will create such havoc and terror in the State that it will be impossible for the government to maintain order and protect the innocent unless harsher punishments are meted out to such criminals. [Publishers]

that they drove off 'Abdullāh[ra] bin Salām, the companion of the Holy Prophet[sa]. In addition, they taunted him with reference to his previous faith saying, *"O son of a Jewess! What have you to do with these matters?"* It is a shame, that the rebels remembered that 'Abdullāh[ra] bin Salām was the son of a Jewish lady, but forgot that he had accepted Islam at the hand of the Holy Prophet[sa]. Furthermore, the Holy Prophet[sa] was immensely pleased when he converted and he too stood by the Holy Prophet[sa] in every hour of difficulty and suffering. Moreover, the rebels also forgot that 'Abdullāh bin Sabā, their leader and instigator – the person who declared Ḥaḍrat 'Alī[ra] to be the *waṣī* of the Holy Prophet[sa] and presented him in opposition to Ḥaḍrat 'Uthmān[ra] – was also the son of a Jewess. In fact, he was a Jew himself and was only outwardly expressing Islam.

THE REBELS ASSASSINATE HADRAT 'UTHMAN[RA]

Disappointed by the rebels, Ḥaḍrat 'Abdullāh bin Salām[ra] left. Upon noticing that it was difficult to murder Ḥaḍrat 'Uthmān[ra] by entering through the door, because the few people who were present on guard there were bent upon killing or dying; so they decided to assassinate Ḥaḍrat 'Uthmān[ra] by jumping over the wall of a neighbouring house. As such, with this intention, a few rebels jumped over the wall of a neighbouring house and sneaked into the room of Ḥaḍrat 'Uthmān[ra]. When these people entered, Ḥaḍrat 'Uthmān[ra] was reciting the Holy Quran. After the siege had been laid, day and night, the only occupation of Ḥaḍrat 'Uthmān[ra] was to offer prayer or recite the Holy Quran, and he would not pay attention to any other work. In those days, the only other task that he performed before the rebels penetrated the house was to appoint two men in order to guard the treasury, because on that night, the Holy Prophet[sa] appeared to him in a vision and said, *"O 'Uthmān[ra]! Break your fast with us this evening."* After this vision, Ḥaḍrat 'Uthmān[ra] was convinced that he would be martyred that day. Hence, taking his responsibility into account, Ḥaḍrat 'Uthmān[ra] ordered two men to stand guard by the gate of the treasury, so that no one would attempt to loot the treasury during the chaos and mischief.

EVENTS LEADING UP TO THE MARTYRDOM OF ḤAḌRAT 'UTHMĀN[RA]

When the rebels reached inside they found Ḥaḍrat 'Uthmān[ra] reciting the Holy Quran. Muḥammad bin Abī Bakr was also among the attackers and due to the power he commanded over the rebels, he considered it his duty to be at the forefront of everything. He advanced and took hold of Ḥaḍrat 'Uthmān[ra] by his beard and gave it a violent tug. In response to this action of his, Ḥaḍrat 'Uthmān[ra] only said this much:

> *"O my brother's son! If your father (Ḥaḍrat Abū Bakr[ra]) had been here now, he would never have done such a thing. What has happened to you? Are you displeased with me for the sake of God? Are you angry at me for anything other than the fact that I have made you fulfil the rights of God?"*

Upon this, Muḥammad bin Abī Bakr turned back in shame. However, the rest of the rebels remained there. Since definite news had been received that the army of Basrah would reach

Madinah that night and this was their last opportunity, the rebels had decided that they would not return without completing their mission. One of them advanced and struck the head of Ḥaḍrat 'Uthmān[ra] with an iron rod. Then he kicked the Quran which was placed opposite Ḥaḍrat 'Uthmān[ra]. The Holy Quran went tumbling towards Ḥaḍrat 'Uthmān[ra] and drops of blood fell upon it from his head. What to talk of dishonouring the Holy Quran – the virtue and honesty of these people became fully exposed by this event.

The verse upon which the blood of Ḥaḍrat 'Uthmān[ra] fell was a magnificent prophecy that was fulfilled in its own time with such grandeur that a person who possessed even the hardest of hearts closed his eyes, out of fear, after beholding a glimpse of its blood stained words. The verse was:

فَسَيَكْفِيكَهُمُ اللّٰهُ ۚ وَهُوَ السَّمِيعُ الْعَلِيمُ

"Allah will surely avenge thee against them, for He is All-Hearing, All-Knowing."[121]

After this a person by the name of Saudān advanced and desired to attack him with a sword. When he made his first strike, Ḥaḍrat 'Uthmān[ra] shielded himself with his hand and his hand was wounded. Upon this, he said, *"By God the Exalted, this was the first hand to write the Holy Quran."* After this, Saudān made a second attack in an attempt to assassinate Ḥaḍrat 'Uthmān[ra] but his wife Nā'ilah moved forward and stepped in between. This evil person, however, did not even hesitate to strike a lady; he attacked and her fingers were severed.

---

121. Al-Baqarah (2:138)

Consequently, she got out of the way. After this, he made another attack upon Ḥaḍrat 'Uthmān[ra] and severely wounded him. Then, in the thought that perhaps he had not yet died and may survive, when Ḥaḍrat 'Uthmān[ra] was writhing in agony and fell unconscious due to the pain of his wounds, this wretched person immediately took to his neck and began to strangle him. This man did not release the neck of Ḥaḍrat 'Uthmān[ra] until his soul departed his physical body and flew to the heavenly world, eagerly accepting the invitation of the Holy Prophet[sa].[122]

اِنَّا لِلّٰهِ وَاِنَّآ اِلَيْهِ رٰجِعُوْنَ

[meaning, surely, to Allah we belong and to Him shall we return].[123]

At first, overwhelmed by the horror of this scene, the wife of Ḥaḍrat 'Uthmān[ra] was unable to speak. She finally called out for help and the people sitting at the door rushed inside. However, any help was now useless; what was to happen had already taken place. When the freed-slave of Ḥaḍrat 'Uthmān[ra] saw the blood-stained sword, which had been used to martyr Ḥaḍrat 'Uthmān[ra], in the hands of Saudān, he was unable to restrain himself. He advanced and severed the head of Saudān with his sword. In turn, one of his [Saudān's] associates killed him. Now the throne of the Islamic Empire was empty of a *Khalīfah*. The people of Madinah deemed further efforts to be futile and all of them returned to their respective homes. After martyring

122. Tārīkhuṭ-Ṭabarī, vol. 5, pp. 176/181-182, Dhikrul-Khabari 'An Qatlihī Wa Kaifa Qutila, Published by Dārul-Fikr, Beirut, 2002 edition [Publishers]

123. Al-Baqarah (2:157) [Publishers]

Ḥaḍrat 'Uthmān[ra] the rebels began to terrorize the members of his household. The wife of Ḥaḍrat 'Uthmān[ra] desired to move away and when she left, a wretched person from among them remarked to his associates, *"Look at the size of her buttocks."*

Undoubtedly, for a respectable man, no matter what religion he belongs to, it is difficult to even fathom that the rebels would express such foul views at a time when they had just martyred the foremost (pioneer) Companion[ra] of the Holy Prophet[sa]; his son-in-law, the King of the Muslim Empire and then, the *Khalīfah* of the time. However, their indecency was so immense that no evil deed was beyond them. These rebels were neither in pursuit of any good objective, nor did their party consist of righteous people. Some of them were admirers of the deceptive, anti-Islam, strange and peculiar teachings of 'Abdullāh bin Sabā, the Jew. Others were fascinated by [the concept of] excessive socialism, rather, Bolshevism. Some were criminals who had served sentences and were looking to spill out their animosity, while others were robbers and bandits, who saw this conflict as a means of fulfilling their ends. In short, their indecency is not surprising. As a matter of fact, it would have been surprising if these people had not behaved in such a manner.

While the rebels were pillaging and plundering, another freed-slave could not restrain himself when he heard the screams and cries of the household of Ḥaḍrat 'Uthmān[ra]. The slave attacked and killed the person who had killed the first slave. At this, they killed him as well. The rebels even took off the jewellery worn by the women and left the house laughing and mocking.

THE REBELS LOOT BAITUL-MĀL

Following this, the rebels made an open announcement to their people that they should head for *baitul-māl* and loot whatever they could lay their hands upon. The guards decided amongst themselves that the rebels should be left to do as they please, since there was nothing but two sacks of money in *baitul-māl*, the *Khalīfah* of the time had been martyred and there was no use in fighting the rebels. The guards threw the keys of *baitul-māl* and left. As such, the rebels went to *baitul-māl*, opened it and looted whatever was stored inside. In this manner, the rebels placed a stamp of attestation upon the fact that they were bandits and robbers, and had no relation with Islam and the Muslims. Is it not surprising that those people who used to raise the objection against Ḥaḍrat 'Uthmān[ra] that he would give funds to those who were undeserving, the first thing they did after his martyrdom was to loot his house and then *baitul-māl*. However, God the Exalted did not allow their desires to be fulfilled in this respect either, because there was nothing more than a small amount of money in *baitul-māl* at the time, which was insufficient to satisfy their greed.

OUTRAGE OF THE COMPANIONS AT THE MARTYRDOM OF ḤAḌRAT 'UTHMĀN[RA]

When news of the martyrdom of Ḥaḍrat 'Uthmān[ra] reached the companions they were devastated. When Ḥaḍrat Zubair[ra] heard this news he said:

إِنَّا لِلّٰهِ وَإِنَّآ إِلَيْهِ رٰجِعُوْنَ

[meaning, surely, to Allah we belong and to Him shall we return].[124]

Then, he said, *"O God have mercy on 'Uthmān*[ra] *and avenge him."*

When he was told that the rebels were now ashamed and felt remorse for what they had done, he retorted, *"This was a conspiracy,"* and then he recited the following verse:

وَحِيلَ بَيْنَهُمْ وَبَيْنَ مَا يَشْتَهُونَ

"God the Exalted placed obstacles in the fulfilment of their desires."[125]

In other words, since there was very little chance that now the wishes of the rebels would materialise and they could see that the entire Muslim world was in fury against them, they were now displaying remorse. When Ḥaḍrat Ṭalḥah[ra] received the news he said the same, *"May God have mercy on 'Uthmān*[ra] *and avenge him and Islam."* When he was told that they were now repentant he said, *"May destruction befall them,"* and he recited this verse:

فَلَا يَسْتَطِيعُونَ تَوْصِيَةً وَّلَآ اِلٰٓى اَهْلِهِمْ يَرْجِعُوْنَ

"They shall not even be able to make a will, and they shall not be able to return to their families."[126]

In the same manner, when Ḥaḍrat 'Alī[ra] received this news he said, *"May Allah the Exalted have mercy on 'Uthmān*[ra] *and appoint a successor after him who is better for us."*

124. Al-Baqarah (2:157) [Publishers]
125. Sabā (34:55)
126. Yā Sīn (36:51)

When he was also told that they were now repentant, he recited the following verse:

كَمَثَلِ الشَّيْطٰنِ اِذْ قَالَ لِلْاِنْسَانِ اكْفُرْ ۚ فَلَمَّا كَفَرَ قَالَ
اِنِّيْ بَرِيْٓءٌ مِّنْكَ اِنِّيْٓ اَخَافُ اللّٰهَ رَبَّ الْعٰلَمِيْنَ

"Their example is of that Satan, who tells the people, 'Disbelieve,' but when they disbelieve, he says, 'I am averse to you; I fear Allah.'"[127]

When the armies that were coming to aid Ḥaḍrat 'Uthmān[ra] learned that he had been martyred, they turned back from distance of only a few miles from Madinah. They did not wish to enter Madinah because their doing was no longer any use to Ḥaḍrat 'Uthmān[ra]; in fact, it was apprehended that conflict may have escalated. Moreover, the Muslims were generally never keen to fight without an Imām.

Now Madinah was in the possession of the rebels and their behaviour during those days was extremely shocking. They had already martyred Ḥaḍrat 'Uthmān[ra] but now they also had an objection with his burial; for three days, he could not be buried. Finally, a group of companions showed courage and buried Ḥaḍrat 'Uthmān[ra] at night. The rebels placed hindrances in the path of these companions as well, but when some of them threatened to fight them fiercely, they gave in. The rebels took

127. Al-Ḥashr (59:17)

the corpses of the two servants of Ḥaḍrat 'Uthmān[ra] and placed them in the jungle and fed them to the dogs.[128]

نَعُوْذُ بِاللّٰہِ مِنْ ذَالِکَ ۔[129]

SUMMARY & OUTCOME OF THE EVENTS DESCRIBED

These are the actual events which transpired in the final days of the *Khilāfat* of Ḥaḍrat 'Uthmān[ra]. After learning of these events, no one can even imagine that Ḥaḍrat 'Uthmān[ra] or the companions had any involvement in these conflicts. The love, devotion and forbearance with which Ḥaḍrat 'Uthmān[ra] served in the last six years of his *Khilāfat* is to his credit. The like of this cannot be found in any other community, except for among the servants of God, the Holy. He selflessly occupied the seat of *Khilāfat* and returned to his True Beloved selflessly. In perilous times when the blood of even the most patient of men boils with rage, Ḥaḍrat 'Uthmān[ra] adopted such a manner that those who were thirsty for his blood could not even find the lamest excuse to kill him. Ultimately, the rebels had to put Ḥaḍrat 'Uthmān[ra] to the sword and in this manner they confessed that they were the oppressors and Ḥaḍrat 'Uthmān[ra] was innocent.

Similarly, it is clearly evident from these events that the

128. * Tārīkhuṭ-Ṭabarī, vol. 5, p. 181, Dhikrul-Khabari 'An Qatlihī Wa Kaifa Qutila, Published by Dārul-Fikr, Beirut, 2002 edition
* Tārīkhuṭ-Ṭabarī, vol. 5, pp. 195-196, Dhikrul-Khabari 'Anil-Mauḍi'illadhī Dufina Fīhi 'Uthmān, Published by Dārul-Fikr, Beirut, 2002 edition [Publishers]

129. We seek refuge with Allah from such a thing. [Publishers]

companions had no objection against the *Khilāfat* of Ḥaḍrat 'Uthmān[ra]. Until the very last breath, they were loyal and even when it was impossible for them to help in any way, putting their own lives in danger they continued to protect Ḥaḍrat 'Uthmān[ra]. These events also establish that neither did the appointment of governors by Ḥaḍrat 'Uthmān[ra] have anything to do with these conflicts, nor was the tyranny of these governors a cause. The allegation against Ḥaḍrat 'Alī[ra], Ḥaḍrat Ṭalḥah[ra] and Ḥaḍrat Zubair[ra] of secretly conspiring, is also absolutely false. All three of these companions strove to remove this conflict with such loyalty and sympathy that even biological brothers cannot match [their efforts], let alone exceed them. The allegation which is levelled against the *anṣār* that they were displeased with Ḥaḍrat 'Uthmān[ra] is false because we see that all the chiefs among the *anṣār* endeavoured to ward off this conflict.

The real cause of this disorder was that upon witnessing that Islam could not be destroyed by overt schemes, the enemies of Islam turned their attention towards hatching secret conspiracies. Using the name of prominent companions, they secretly began to create factions among the Muslims. The means that they had employed have now become manifest to the people. The rebels persuaded criminals who had served sentences to join them and bribed robbers. They weakened the administration of the State by spreading false concepts of equality. They weakened the faith of people under the guise of religion and prepared a community through thousands of schemes and tactics. Then, through lies, fabrication and deception, these people created such circumstances that it became difficult for Ḥaḍrat 'Uthmān[ra] and the other companions to resist. We know not what the outcome would have been, but from the events we know this much, even if it had been the *Khilāfat* of Ḥaḍrat 'Umar[ra], this conflict still would have arisen; the allegations which were levelled against Ḥaḍrat 'Uthmān[ra] would also have been levelled against Ḥaḍrat 'Umar[ra]; for Ḥaḍrat 'Uthmān[ra] did nothing which Ḥaḍrat 'Umar[ra] and Ḥaḍrat Abū Bakr[ra] had not done.

Due to a shortage of time, since the events of the *Khilāfat* of Ḥaḍrat 'Alī[ra] were mentioned in only a few minutes and were very brief; hence, I deleted this part during my second reading.

AN IMPORTANT NOTE

The following abbreviations have been used. Readers are urged to recite the full salutations when reading the book:

sa *ṣallallāhu ʿalaihi wa sallam*, meaning 'may the peace and blessings of Allah be upon him' is written after the name of the Holy Prophet Muḥammad[sa].

as *ʿalaihissalām*, meaning 'on whom be peace' is written after the name of Prophets other than the Holy Prophet Muḥammad[sa].

ra *raḍiyallāhu ʿanhu/ʿanhā/ʿanhum*, meaning 'may Allah be pleased with him/her/them' is written after the names of the Companions of the Holy Prophet Muḥammad[sa] or of the Promised Messiah[as].

aa *ayyadahullāhu taʿālā binaṣrihil-ʿAzīz*, meaning 'may Allah the Almighty help him with his powerful support' is written after the name of the present Head of the Ahmadiyya Muslim Jamāʿat, Ḥaḍrat Mirza Masroor Ahmad, Khalīfatul-Masīḥ V[aa].

In transliterating Arabic words we have followed the following system adopted by the Royal Asiatic Society.

ا at the beginning of a word, pronounced as *a, i, u* preceded by a very slight aspiration, like *h* in the English word 'honour'.

ث *th*, pronounced like *th* in the English word '*thing*'.

ح *ḥ*, a guttural aspirate, stronger than *h*.

خ *kh*, pronounced like the Scotch *ch* in '*loch*'.

ذ *dh*, pronounced like the English *th* in '*that*'.

ص *ṣ*, strongly articulated *s*.

ض *ḍ*, similar to the English *th* in '*this*'.

ط *ṭ*, strongly articulated palatal *t*.

ظ *ẓ*, strongly articulated *z*.

ع ', a strong guttural, the pronunciation of which must be learnt by the ear.

غ *gh*, a sound approached very nearly in the *r* '*grasseye*' in French, and in the German *r*. It requires the muscles of the throat to be in the 'gargling' position whilst pronouncing it.

ق *q*, a deep guttural *k* sound.

ء ', a sort of catch in the voice.

Short vowels are represented by:

a for ــَــ (like *u* in '*bud*')

i for ــِــ (like *i* in '*bid*')

u for ــُــ (like *oo* in '*wood*')

Long vowels by:

ā for ــٰــ or آ (like *a* in '*father*');

ī for ی ــِــ or ــٖــ (like *ee* in '*deep*');

ū for و ــُــ (like *oo* in '*root*');

Other:

ai for ی ــَــ (like *i* in '*site*');

au for و ——َ—— (resembling *ou* in '*sound*')

The consonants not included in the above list have the same phonetic value as in the principal languages of Europe. Curved commas are used in the system of transliteration, ' for ع , ' for ء. We have not transliterated Arabic words which have become part of English language, e.g., Islam, Quran, Hadith, Mahdi, jihad, Ramadan, ummah, etc. The Royal Asiatic Society rules of transliteration for names of persons, places and other terms, could not be followed throughout the book as many of the names contain non-Arabic characters and carry a local transliteration and pronunciation style which in itself is also not consistent either.

The abbreviation A.H. represents the renowned Islamic calendar system, which began after the migration of the Holy Prophet[sa] to Madinah, and means, '*After Hijrah*'.

GLOSSARY

Ahl-e-Bait—A term which refers to the household members of the Holy Prophet[sa] and literally means, 'people of the house.'

Aḥmadiyya Muslim Jamā'at—The Community of Muslims who have accepted the claims of Ḥaḍrat Mirzā Ghulām Aḥmad[as] of Qadian as the Promised Messiah and Mahdi. The Community was established by Ḥaḍrat Mirzā Ghulām Aḥmad[as] in 1889, and is now under the leadership of his fifth *Khalīfah*—Ḥaḍrat Mirza Masroor Ahmad (may Allah be his help). The Community is also known as **Jamā'at-e-Aḥmadiyya**. A member of the Community is called an **Aḥmadī Muslim** or simply an **Aḥmadī**.

Allah—Allah is the personal name of God in Islam. To show proper reverence to Him, Muslims often add *Ta'ālā*, translated here as 'the Exalted', when saying His Holy name.

Āmīn—May Allah make it so.

Anṣār—Literally means 'the Helpers' and was a title of veneration given to the Muslims of Madinah on account of their giving protection to the Holy Prophet[sa] and his companions when they migrated from Makkah to Madinah due to persecution.

'Asharah Mubashsharah—This is a term which means, *'the ten who have been given glad tidings'.* In actuality, *'asharah mubashsharah* has become a renowned term to refer to ten people about whom the Holy Prophet[sa] had prophecied entrance into paradise. However, there were many more such companions who were also granted this glad tiding. Therefore, in actuality, the term specifically refers to those ten *muhājirin*, who were a part of the *majlis-e-shūrā* [consultative body] of the Holy Prophet[sa] and who he especially trusted.

As-Sābiqūnal-Awwalūn—A term used in the Holy Quran, in Sūrah At-Taubah (9:100), which means, 'the foremost among the believers.'

Azwāj-e-Mutahharāt—A title of honour for the noble wives of the Holy Prophet[sa] and literally means, 'spouses who have been purified.'

Bai'at—An oath of allegience to a religious leader; initiation at the hands of a Prophet or his *Khalīfah*. Literally means 'to be sold.'

Baitul-Māl—The National Treasury of the Islamic State.

Ghazwah—A military expedition in which the Holy Prophet[sa] participated himself.

Hajjatul-Wadā'—The last hajj performed by the Holy Prophet[sa] prior to his demise and literally means, 'the farewell hajj.'

Ḥaḍrat—A term of respect used for a person of established righteousness and piety.

Hadith—A saying of the Holy Prophet Muḥammad[sa]. The plural is *aḥādith*.

Hijrah—The migration of the Holy Prophet[sa] to Madinah, due to persecution in his homeland, Makkah.

Holy Prophet[sa]—A term used exclusively for the Founder of Islam, Ḥaḍrat Muḥammad, may peace and blessings of Allah be upon him.

Holy Quran—The Book sent by Allah for the guidance of mankind. It was revealed word by word to the Holy Prophet Muḥammad[sa] over a period of twenty-three years.

'Iddat—A fixed time period specified by the Islamic shariah, which must elapse before a widow or divorced lady can marry again.

Jāhiliyyah—Refers to the pre-Islamic era prior to the advent of the Holy Prophet[sa] and literally means, 'ignorance.'

Jamā'at—*Jamā'at* means community. Although the word *jamā'at* itself may refer to any community, in this book, *Jamā'at* specifically refers to the Aḥmadiyya Muslim Jamā'at.

Jihad—The literal meaning of this word is 'striving'. The term is used to mean self-purification as well as religious wars in some instances.

Khalīfah and Khilāfat—Caliph is derived from the Arabic word *Khalīfah*, which herein means the successor. *Khulafā'* is the plural of *Khalīfah*. In Islamic terminology, the title *'Khalīfa-e-Rāshid'* [Rightly Guided *Khalīfah*] is applied to one of the first four *khulafā'* who continued the mission of the Holy Prophet Muḥammad[sa]. Aḥmadī Muslims refer to each successor of the Promised Messiah[as] as *Khalīfatul-Masīḥ*. The institution of successorship is called *Khilāfat*.

Khalīfatul-Masīḥ II—Ḥaḍrat Khalīfatul-Masīḥ II, Mirza Bashir-ud-Din Mahmud Ahmad[ra] (1889–1965), was the second successor of the Promised Messiah[as]. He is also called Muṣliḥ-e-Mau'ūd because he was born in accordance with the prophecy made by the Promised Messiah[as] in 1886 concerning the birth of a righteous son who would be endowed with unique abilities and attributes.

Khalīfatul-Masīḥ V—Ḥaḍrat Khalīfatul-Masīḥ V, Mirza Masroor Ahmad[aa], is the fifth successor of the Promised

Messiah[as] and the current Imam of Jamā'at-e-Aḥmadiyya. He is the great grandson of the Promised Messiah[as].

Khilāfat—The institution of successorship in Islam. See also **Khalīfah.**

Khātamul-Anbiyā'—A title of the Holy Prophet[sa], which means, 'Seal of the Prophets' due to his unparalleled status.

Khātamul-Auṣiyā'—A title of Ḥaḍrat 'Alī[ra] given to him by those who believe him to be the *waṣī* of the Holy Prophet[sa]. See also *waṣī*.

Madīnah Munawwarah—Literally means 'Madinah, the Enlightened' and is a title of honour used to lovingly refer to the city of Madinah. When the Holy Prophet[sa] migrated from Makkah due to persecution he settled in Madinah.

Majlis-e-Shūrā—A consultative body, which offers suggestions in matters of importance.

Makkah Mukarramah—Literally means 'Makkah, the Honoured' and is a title of reverence used to lovingly refer to the city of Makkah. This is the blessed city where the Holy Prophet[sa] was born and where he made his claim to prophethood after receiving revelation from Allah the Exalted.

Manzil—A distance equivalent to 19 miles or 25 kilometers.

Masjid-e-Nabawī—The famous mosque built by the Holy Prophet[sa] when he migrated to Madīnah, and literally means 'The Prophet's Mosque'.

Muḥammad—Proper name of the Prophet of Islam.

The Promised Messiah—This term refers to the Founder of the Aḥmadiyya Muslim Jamā'at, Ḥaḍrat Mirzā Ghulām Aḥmad[as] of Qadian. He claimed that he had been sent by Allah in accordance with the prophecies of the Holy Prophet[sa] about the coming of *al-Imam al-Mahdi* (the Guided Leader) and Messiah.

Qaṣr—A shortened version of the obligatory prayer [*ṣalāt*], which is offered as such in certain circumstances.

Raj'at—The belief that those who have passed away among the Prophets would return to the world again with their physical bodies.

Rajaz—A specific meter in Arabic poetry, which contains a discourse in rhyme. This word also denotes the recitation of poetic verse in general.

Rak'at—A cycle in the formal Muslim prayer and the plural of this word is *rak'āt*.

Ṣadaqah—Almsgiving in Islam to assist the poor and needy. However, the Holy Prophetsa has mentioned that *ṣadaqah* can be given in various forms, even by meeting another person with a cheerful face. The term, therefore, is very broad in meaning, and has many inferences. In this lecture, on page 63 the word has also been used in the context of 'forgiveness.'

Sūrah—A term in Arabic referring to a chapter of the Holy Quran.

Sunnah—Practice of the Holy Prophet[sa]

Takbīr—To proclaim the greatness of Allah, saying *Allāhu Akbar*, which means, *'Allah is the Greatest.'*

Ummahātul-Mu'minīn—A term of respect and reverence for the wives of the Holy Prophet[sa] and literally means, 'the mothers of the believers.'

'Umrah—A lesser Pilgrimage to the Holy Ka'bah in which some of the rites of the hajj are left out. *'umrah* can be performed at any time during the year.

Waṣī—Literally this word has many meanings, which include, 'a testator, gaurdian, custodian, keeper, or administrator' However, in the context of the subject discussed in this book, it is a title given to Ḥaḍrat 'Alī[ra] by a group of Muslims who believe that he was meant to be the first *Khalīfah* after the demise of the Holy Prophet[sa] and that the Holy Prophet[sa] had bequethed him this office prior to his demise.

INDEX

'Abdullāh bin Sabā
arrives in Egypt 39
attempted to take advantage of the absence of provincial governors 67
converted to Islam in order to create rifts among Muslims 30
declares 'Alī bin Abī Ṭālib[ra] to be the *waṣī* of the Holy Prophet 45
exploits Abū Dharr Ghifārī[ra] 33
forms a party 31
goes to Basrah 31
makes Egypt his headquarters 40
possessed extraordinary intelligence and judgement 55
preached of a physical re-advent of Holy Prophet[sa] 44
sets out with rebels for Madinah in a final attempt to achieve his objective 84
sows seed of disorder in Kufah 32
spreads his views by sending agents to other states 55
toured all the Muslim states 31
undertook a dangerous scheme in order to defame governors 56
was a Jew 30
was the driving force behind the disorders 30, 41

'Abdullāh bin Salām[ra]
forbade the rebels from killing Ḥaḍrat 'Uthmān[ra] 139
heard taunt from the rebels 140

'Abdullāh bin Saraḥ
sent news to Ḥaḍrat 'Uthmān[ra] of the caravan and their intentions 84
was the governor of Egypt 84

'Abdullāh bin 'Umar[ra]
high status of, 59
sent as a delgate to Syria 57
was well suited to be sent to Syria 59

'Abdur-Raḥmān bin Khālid[ra]
attempts to reform the rebels from Kufah 53
was the governor of Jazīrah 53

Abū Bakr Ṣiddīq[ra]
Muslims unified in the era of 8

Abu Dharr Ghifārī[ra]
confronts Mu'āwiyah 34
falls victim to Ibni Saudā's deception 34
summoned in Madinah 36
viewed the accumulation of wealth as being unlawful 33
was innocent 37

Abū Mūsā Al-Ash'arī[ra]
gathered the people of Kufah and admonished them 74
is appointed as the governor of Kufah 72, 74
refused to lead the prayers 75

Abū Shuraiḥ[ra]
sells his wealth and returns to Madinah 30
testifies against the robbers 29

'Ā'ishah Ṣiddīqah[ra]
did not consider it appropriate to remain in Madinah 120

'Alī bin Abī Ṭālib[ra]
counterfeit letters were falsly written on behalf of, 105
devoted all his efforts to bring an end to Ḥaḍrat 'Uthmān's[ra] suffering 127
did not conspire in order to acquire *khilāfat* 11, 149
plainly rejected having written any letters to the rebels of Kufah 106
rebuked the rebels of Egypt 88
was severe in restricting the disorder 18

Allegations, Rebuttal to
Ḥaḍrat 'Uthmān[ra] appointed young men as governors 80
Ḥaḍrat 'Uthmān[ra] did not shorten prayer while on a journey 79
Ḥaḍrat 'Uthmān[ra] introduced the innovation of establishig public pastures 80

'Ammār bin Yāsir[ra]
'Abdullāh bin Sabā welcomes 61
only person from among the companions to be deceived by the rebels 62
took no part in the rebellion 114
was delayed and no news came from him 58, 61
was mislead due to inexperience in political affairs 61, 62, 114
was sent as a delegate to Egypt 61

Basrah
people of, at the forefront of creating disorder 41

Companions
did not usurp the rights of others 15
formed two groups in order to restore order 127
fought the rebels outside Ḥaḍrat 'Uthmān's[ra] house 130
greatly detested the rebels 82, 85
had prepared Muslims for jihad in all the Muslim states against the rebels 129
held state authority and received a speacial share of the riches 12
immaculate character of 3
left in a dilema, weather to fight the rebels or not, on account of Ḥaḍrat 'Uthmān's[ra] instruction 132
lofty status of, 14
never hoarded wealth 35
prayed for Ḥaḍrat 'Uthmān[ra] to be avenged 146

received direct training from Holy Prophet[sa] 76
sacrifice of, exceeded that of others 15
some injured while fighting the rebels 137
strongly felt that the rebels should be executed 81
superiority of, criticised 27
the children of, gaurded Ḥaḍrat 'Uthmān[ra] house 128
were loyal to *Khilāfat* 148

Disorder
real cause of, 149

Dissension
causes of,
due to a lack of spiritual training the initial enthusiasm died down 19, 23
jealousy towards the companions 12, 17
lack of education of the large number of new entrants into Islam 19, 23
new entrants into Islam were unfamiliar with the Arabic language 23
opponents outwardly accepted Islam with the hope of destroying it 21
some individuals misused the freedom which Islam afforded them 17
trend of questioning those in authority 17
foundation laid fifteen years after the demise of Holy Prophet[sa] 2
no sign of, six years into Ḥaḍrat 'Uthmān's[ra] *khilāfat* 25
was the result of a secret conspiracy hatched by the Jews 60

Egypt
an ideal place for 'Abdullah bin Sabā 39

Ḥakīm bin Jabalah
agent of Ibnus-Saudā 44
was a robber under house arrest 31

Ḥasan bin 'Alī[ra]
fought the rebels while reciting *rajaz* 135

Ḥimrān bin Abbān
married a women during her *'iddat* 28

History
incidents of, must fit into a sequence of events 91
narrations of, not as reliable as *aḥādīth* 91

Holy Prophet[ra], the
spiritual power of 6

Investigative Committee
all report back of peace and tranquility in the Islamic states 57
all returned, except Ammār bin Yāsir[ra] 58
members of, were men of high calibre 58, 59
sent to enquire weather provincial governors were unjust 57

Islam
offered freedom of conscience and action 17

spread so rapidly that its opponents were unable to preceive this 20

Islamic history
destorted by Europeans due to conflicting narrations 92
hidden aspects disclosed 3
people of this era unaware of 3

Islamic States
condition of the residents of, testimony of Ibnus-Saudā'ṣ deputy 39

Khilāfat
not a worldly government 14
the progress of Islam associated with 21

Kufah
people of, at the forefront of creating disorder 41, 67

Lahore Islamiyyah College
established a historical society 1

Madinah
people of, caught off guard by the rebels 92
people of, unable to fight the rebels 93, 107
residents of, form their army in two groups 86

Mālikul-Ashtar
incites people against Sa'īd bin Al-'Āṣ[ra] on entring Kufah 69
many influenced by lies of, 73
reached Kufah in no time 69
sought forgiveness from 'Uthmān[ra] was unable to keep his repentance in tact 69

Marwān
could not have been responsible for forging the letter 103

Mu'āwiyah[ra]
attempts to reform the exiled rebels from Kufah 50
held a position of great awe upon the residents of Syria 59
makes four prepositions to Ḥaḍrat 'Uthmān[ra] 65
sends the rebels back to Kufah 53
was attacked by rebels 52
was managing the affairs of State with excellence 32

Mughīrah bin Al-Akhnas[ra]
killed while fighting the rebels 137

Muḥammad bin Abī Bakr
grabbed Ḥaḍrat 'Uthmān[ra] by his beard 141
held no religious merit 46, 113
partook in the disorder 46
was arrogant and thought himself above the law 78

Muḥammad bin Abī Ḥudhaifah
an orphan brought up by Ḥaḍrat 'Uthmān[ra] 46
introduction to 113

Muḥammad bin Maslamah[ra]
sent as a delegate to Kufah 57
was a venerable companion of great influence 59

Muḥammad bin Ṭalḥah[ra]
recited *rajaz* while fighting the rebels 135

Muḥammad, the Messenger of Allah
a so-called Muslim objects to his distribution of wealth 17
ordered the executuion of anyone who created disacord in the presence of an Imām 75

Muslim Converts
band of youths form in order to commit robberies 28
habit of commiting sins re-emerges 27, 30
initial enthusiasm declines 27

Qa'qā' bin 'Amr
was the officer of the military post in Kufah 67
arrived to arrest Yazid bin Qais 67

Rebels, the
all three carvans of, could not have possibly reached Madinah so quickly 99
army of, employed a new strategy 90
army of, sent two men to ascertain the circumstances 86
began to openly express their views 47
could not openly rebel in the prsence of Ḥaḍrat 'Uthmān[ra] 61
did not allow Sa'īd bin Al-'Āṣ[ra] enter Kufah on his return 71
differed on who they wanted to be *Khalīfah* 87
exiled from Kufah towards Syria 49
expressed foul views regarding the wife of Ḥaḍrat 'Uthmān[ra] 143
fabricated story of intercepting a letter off a suspicious messenger 95, 102
gained full control over the administration of Madinah 116
gave Ḥaḍrat 'Uthmān[ra] three options 124
grew restless and were in wait of an excuse to martyr Ḥaḍrat 'Uthmān[ra] 125
had no connection with Islam 110
had produced many counterfeit letters previously 105
immense indecency of, 144
jump into Ḥaḍrat 'Uthmān's[ra] house from a neighbouring house 140
kill a servant of Ḥaḍrat 'Uthmān[ra] 143
killed the servant of Sa'īd bin Al-'Āṣ[ra] 71
martyr Ḥaḍrat 'Uthmān[ra] 143
openly criticized Ḥaḍrat 'Uthmān[ra] and Sa'īd[ra] 48
order Ḥaḍrat Mu'āwiyah[ra] to step down from his office 52
plan of suddenly occupying Madinah frustrated 74
tried to prevent the burial of Ḥaḍrat 'Uthmān[ra] 147
proved that they were robbers and looters 145
real objective of, was the destruction of the Islamic government 76
real opposition of, was against Ḥaḍrat 'Uthmān[ra] 73

revealed their plan to Ḥaḍrat 'Uthmān's[ra] informants 77
revealed they had three supporters in Madinah 77
secretly incited people against the companions 27
seek permission to enter Madinah 87
sent a delegation of a few people from each province to question Ḥaḍrat 'Uthmān[ra] 77
set a fire outside Ḥaḍrat 'Uthmān's[ra] door 134
set out to occupy Madinah and take charge of the government 84
settled at three seperate places outside Madinah 86
suddenly laid siege on Madinah 93
threatened the people of Madinah 94
told lies and slandered others contrary to Islamic teaching 72
two reasons for their boldness and daring behaviour 85
were well aware that killing Ḥaḍrat 'Uthmān[ra] was not lawful under any circumstances 138

Religious movement
is different from a worldly state 13

Robbers
attempt to rob a house 28
executed on an open plain outside Kufah 29, 41
parents of, seek revenge from Walīd bin 'Utbah 41

Sabā'īs
were supporters of 'Abdullāh bin Sabā 67

Sa'īd bin Al-'Āṣ[ra]
appointed as the governor of Kufah 44
forgives the perpetrators 48
held an open gathering 47
rebels beat a young man in the presence of 47
turned away by rebels on his return from Madinah 71

'Umar bin Al-Juraid
was the acting governor for Sa'īd bin Al-'Āṣ[ra] in his absence 70

'Umar bin Al-Khaṭṭāb[ra]
allegation levelled against 18
had identified the root cause of the conflict 24
Muslims unified in the era of 8

Ummi Ḥabībah[ra]
attempted to safeguard the wills of orphans and widows 118

Usāmah bin Zaid[ra]
high status of 58
sent as a delegate to Basrah 57

'Uthmān bin 'Affān[ra]
accepted Islam through Abū Bakr[ra] 8
appointed and sent 'Abdullāh bin 'Abbās as the *amīr* of hajj 125
appointment as *Khalīfah* of, 8
did not openly charge the rebels of deceit on account of his humility and modesty 98

drops of blood fell from the head of, onto a verse of the Holy Quran 141
forgave the rebels despite the verdict of execution by the companions 79
heart rendering message of, read out before the pilgrims in Makkah 129
held a special rank of honour in the sight of the Holy Prophet[sa] 8
held fast to the rope of Islamic unity despite his old age 60
held in admiration in initial years of his *khilāfat* 25
ordered the companions not to fight the rebels 111
possessed rare moral qualities even prior to Islam 10
refused to step down from the office of *khilāfat* 115, 138
requested for aid as the rebels had cut off his water supply 117
requests provincial governors for aid 121
sent a delegation to various states for enquiry 57
sentences a band of robbers to death 29
sent to the Makkans to negotiate with them 9
summons provincial governors 64
turns down Ḥaḍrat Mu'āwiyah's[ra] proposals 65
two daughters of the Holy Prophet[sa] wedded to, 8
valued the single negative report received from the delegation 63
was certain of his martyrdom that day 140
was not concerned for his personal well bieng; his only concern was for Islam 128
was not responsible for the disorder 24, 148
wrote a letter to the various Islamic states reagrding the reports of disturbance 63

Walīd bin 'Utbah
house of, besieged 41
rebels plot to disgrace 42
summoned to Madinah and lashed 43
was the governor of Kufah 41

Yazīd bin Qais
anounced that Ḥaḍrat 'Uthmān should be removed from the office of *khilāfat* 67
Qa'qā' bin 'Amr arrived to arrest 67
was the leader of the Sabā'īs in Kufah 68
wrote a letter calling the exiled rebels of Kufah 68